A SMALL GARDEN DESIGNER'S *HANDBOOK*

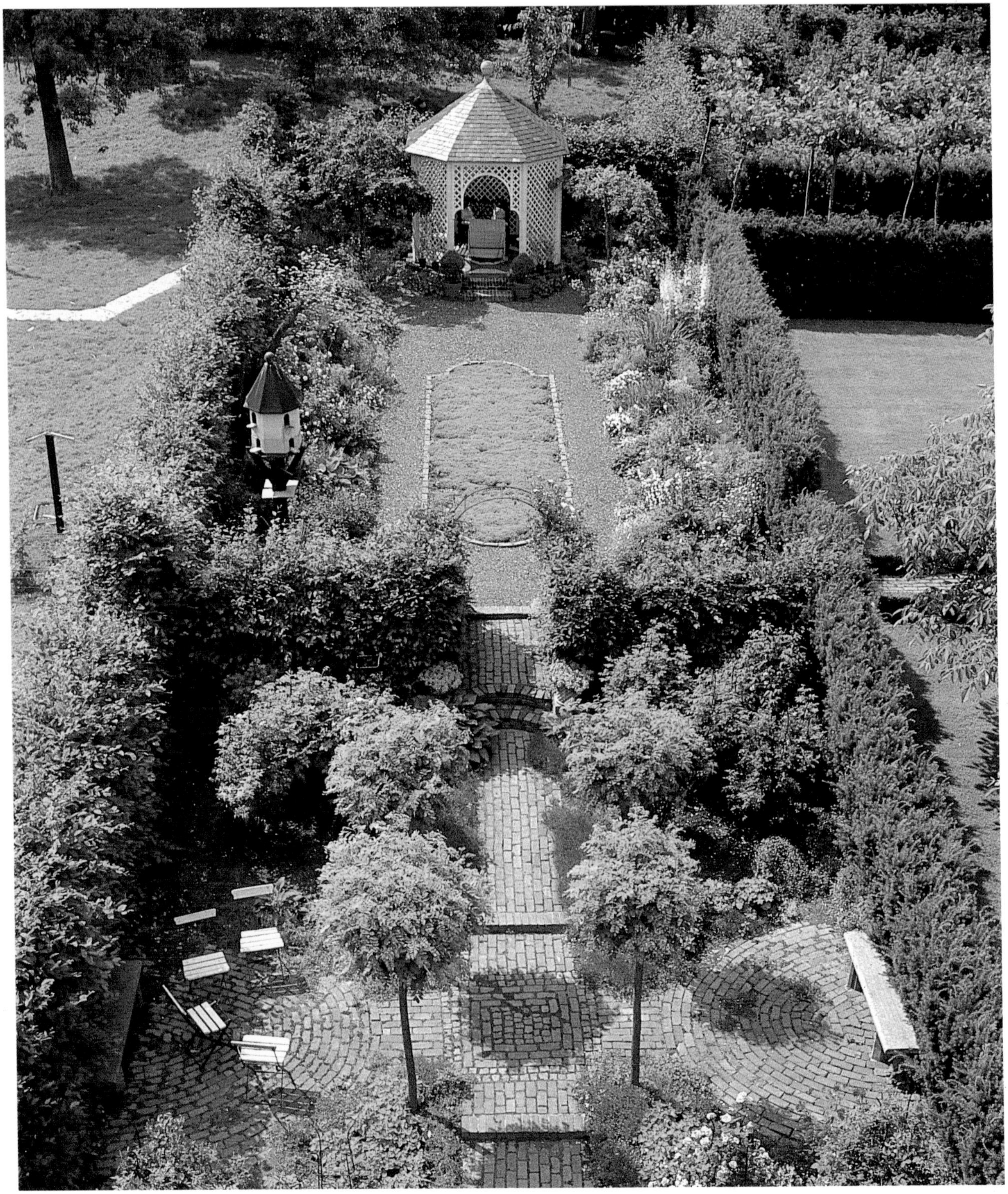

A
SMALL GARDEN
DESIGNER'S
HANDBOOK

ROY STRONG

conran
OCTOPUS

This book grew out of *Creating Small Gardens* and is, in a way, complementary to it. Once again it is specifically design orientated, providing a much needed discourse on the design features open to those planning a small garden. In compiling it, I am indebted, in many matters horticultural, to the guidance and knowledge of David Joyce. Christine Robbins' and Sally Hynard's illustrations prove that such drawings can not only be pertinent and practical but, at the same time, a delight.

Roy Strong

Half title Luxuriant growth can soften the severity of formal outline and shapes without undermining the structure of a garden.
Frontispiece This small garden demonstrates how many factors contribute to good design. Sensitive allocation of space has been accentuated by slight but well-considered changes of level.

First published in 1987 by
Conran Octopus Limited
37 Shelton Street
London WC2H 9HN

First published in paperback in 1990
Reprinted 1990, 1991, 1992 (thrice), 1993, 1995

This paperback edition published in 1997

Editors Mary Davies and Mary Trewby
Contributing editor Caroline Boisset
Art Director Douglas Wilson
Designer Prue Bucknall
Picture Research Shona Wood and Nadine Bazar
Production Jill Embleton
Illustrators Christine Robbins and Sally Hynard/
   The Garden Studio

ISBN 1 85029 815 7

Typeset by MS Filmsetting Limited, Frome

Printed in China

CONTENTS

INTRODUCTION

No one has yet written a classic on small-garden design. The nearest we have got to it is Gertrude Jekyll's and Laurence Weaver's *Gardens for Small Country Houses*, published in 1912. That intimated that the spacious days of the great country house gardens were drawing to an end. In the aftermath of the Great War, gardens shrank to an acre or two and the armies of gardeners diminished along with them to a mere handful. No one, however, could forsee that after the Second World War gardeners were virtually to vanish as a breed or that gardens were to shrink at an even more radical rate.

What, in fact, happened simultaneously was a vast expansion of owner-occupied houses with small gardens, symptomatic of a more egalitarian society. Unfortunately, the traditions of garden design were not carried over; 'design' was seen as the prerogative of those lucky enough to own large gardens. But the true art of garden-making is too important – and too exciting – to be allowed to die.

Most of us live in detached, semi-detached or terrace houses with a small rectangular garden around or at the back and front. This means that the art of garden design is especially challenging, particularly now when so many more people who occupy such houses are conscious of how closely related good design is to efficient and enjoyable living. I find it very depressing that so little practical design help is available for those who want to transform their gardens in the same way that they are able to change the interiors of houses through the availability of design magazines and of chain stores with ranges of coordinated furnishings, fabrics and wallpapers. By comparison, the average garden centre is no help, nor are the gardening magazines which focus too much on rare plants and the problems of horticulture.

So we stand at the crossroads in small garden design, with enormous opportunities for those with the imagination to take the leap away from the familiar clichés. And away from the influential design philosophy of the 1950s, which extolled the virtues of the landscape style of the eighteenth century, with its manicuring of nature into undulations and curves, with its use of bold plantings of greenery, whether trees or shrubs, its deployment of winding paths and irregularly shaped lakes and ponds. Thirty years on, we can see the unhappy results of this in the majority of suburban gardens, where what was appropriate for a 100-acre park surrounding a Palladian mansion has ludicrously been miniaturized into a suburban rectangle. If Capability Brown could return from the grave he would be quite shattered to witness such a total misapplication of his principles of garden design!

In order to go forwards from this, however, it is necessary to go back. In compiling this book, I have been keenly aware that I was picking up a tradition of garden writing which stretched back to the sixteenth century. Books of the past recorded and illustrated existing gardens and included many ideas for features, such as designs for summer houses or parterres or how to train plants into interesting shapes. Old books on gardening and those that illustrate old gardens are an inspiration and I have spent many fruitful hours looking through library collections. Working in this way, I have set out to compile a series of options of the kind which always used to be available and which are easy to adapt to the much smaller cultivated areas of our own day. This does not mean that my approach is in the least archaeological or antiquarian. The needs of the last decades of this century have been borne in mind and the resulting gardens, made as they are for today, are far from being mere historical curiosities.

Design features can be expensive or cheap, immediate or long term. A stone wall or a gazebo demands a heavy financial outlay but will provide instant effect and life-long satisfaction. Elegant pergolas and arbours can be made from inexpensive larch poles and trellis, giving just as much delight, but they will be transitory. A splendid statue or garden ornament also gives instantaneous substance and identity to a garden. Other design features, however, will present horticultural challenges and call for patience. It will take a decade to achieve a really splendid yew hedge and as long to train topiary to any size. But when the project reaches fruition the garden will contain something utterly unique which can be displayed with pride. In any case, there is a great deal of pleasure to be had purely in the process of creating these effects.

Inevitably, the question raised is: how do you start? That question has determined the structure of this book. I take the first-time gardener through what, at times, may seem a daunting experience – it is also often exhilarating – deciding how to lay out and design a garden that is really beautiful, original and a vivid reflection of the essential personality of its owner.

That process begins with basic planning, allocating the available space. After that you will need to consider the approaches and entrances to the garden as well as its division by way of hedges, fences and walls into different areas, features which are essentially structural. The rest of the book considers in sequence features which embellish this framework in terms of design – everything from plant containers to pleaching, from the training of fruit trees to the placing of containers, and concludes with exhaustive lists of suggestions for planting.

But let us return to that vital question, how do you start? The point of departure must be what is already there. Look down on the garden from an upstairs window or from a terrace overlooking the garden – examine closely what you see. If you have a camera, take snapshots and have some large prints made, preferably repeating that process through the seasons. You must begin from a very basic premise. Is what is there what you want to see? Is it interesting to look at or dull? Have you strong feelings, negative or positive, about items in the garden; do you, for instance, feel impelled to rush out with an axe and fell a copper beech whose dark leaves cast a funereal pall of gloom over the garden? It is useful to do a rough sketch of the area, take measurements and plot all the existing features, and then work it up to scale on graph paper. You might use a second colour to note what you really do not like and wish to get rid of – include both plants and artefacts.

Walk around the garden asking the same sort of questions, a process which should be repeated from every window that looks out on to the garden. In the case of a front garden, go right outside the territorial limits of the property and look back at it from various viewpoints. Do not be entirely inward looking. It may be that your garden should be designed as a foil, leading the eye to something completely outside it, such as an old church, an orchard or some marvellous view.

The camera can be a superb recorder; it is a particular joy if you take pictures from the same vantage points over several years, thus documenting the garden's transformation. It is well worth starting a loose-leaf file. You can put into it everything from plans to nursery bills, annotating it as the garden develops and changes. There is no surer corrective to the view that it takes decades to make a garden. For the real enthusiast, a garden diary will be a must, recording, season by season, the weather and what is done when, even if only in the most cursory way. Within a few years, these records will have become quite absorbing as your plan grows towards fulfilment. And even if you move house, you will have a record of the triumphs and tribulations to look back upon and from which to learn.

In doing this preliminary survey, it is important to plot the movement of the sun and of the prevailing winds. Charting the course of the sun calls for a full year's observation, because the amount of shade cast in winter differs considerably from that in the summer. Sun and light, as well as the soil, will affect what you can and cannot plant. (Soil analysis kits are available from garden centres; whether your soil is dry or wet is easy enough to observe, but whether it is acid or alkaline calls for chemistry. The results will certainly condition your choice of plants and their rate of growth.)

Once you know the sunny areas, you will be able to site a summerhouse or an arbour to enjoy its warmth. Equally, it will determine the placing of fruit trees for ripening and, in the case of sun-loving plants, the positioning of flowerbeds. Those areas discovered to be in the shade will call for shade-tolerant shrubs and plants and, in addition, ones which lighten the gloom with their pale foliage and white and creamy blossoms. Watch, too, what happens to the garden after heavy rainfall. If it remains waterlogged for a long time after, drains will have to be installed.

Armed with all this information, you are now in a position to decide the style and layout of your garden. Initially, this calls for making up your mind whether there is enough

space for more than one garden room and, if so, what each will contain. Apportion the areas on the plan.

You have now reached the stage where you will need to consider the available repertory of garden features which could be included in your scheme, those which you want and you have room to include. The choice will certainly be affected by another decision, whether you wish the garden to be formal and symmetrical, or informal. If you have enough space you may be able to accommodate both styles in separate areas. Combining the two in the same space will only result in disaster.

In designing the layout, always approach it in a spirit of adventure, enjoyment and also patience. Be bold and never be put off by gloom-mongering friends who tell you that you will never live to see the fruits of your creation. Even the making of the garden will give untold pleasure.

Remember, it is perfectly valid to look for a low-maintenance garden with plants that virtually look after themselves. Not everyone can afford to spend long hours in the garden or in the study of plants. In any case, garden

Garden and house must form an harmonious whole. Here a terrace links the house interior with the outdoors, an informal scattering of containers helping to blur the division. The walls of the house carry climbers and wall shrubs so that architecture and garden blend. The garden itself has a formal structure with box-edged flowerbeds.

design through the ages has always allowed for beautiful gardens to be created from the simplest ingredients, such as a paved area filled with a scattering of containers and surrounded by a clipped evergreen hedge. Even if your aim is to turn your small garden into a horticultural paradise, it does not necessarily mean that in design terms your garden will be better. It will only be different.

GROUND PLANNING

Garden design, as it developed in the Renaissance, was based on the fact that the earth's surface could be re-ordered by the superimposition of paths, steps, plants, water and buildings. The patterns made were intended as much to be looked down upon as traversed on foot. We forget that most gardens in the past were meant to be viewed from above, looking out through upper-floor windows or from the top of a flight of steps or a terrace – knot gardens and parterres, for instance, were planted in the form of mazes, coats of arms or sinuous arabesque patterns. Visiting any great garden today you will often find yourself on a terrace at the top of a flight of steps made so it is possible to view the garden below in terms of pattern – paths, beds and flowers – before you descend and walk through it. This approach is equally valid for the smallest spaces, many of which are town gardens seen from a first-floor window or from a raised terrace.

When considering an existing garden in terms of pattern, you need to assess what is already there. Are the shapes of the paths, beds and changes of level of good proportion or should the space be adjusted and reallocated? Is there an agreeable mixture of materials underfoot in the way of stone, brick, concrete slabs and grass? Are the paths going where you want them to and do they form an attractive design? Do essential entries, exits and service points, such as a garage or toolshed, have suitable paths that are wide and direct enough for convenient access?

You should begin by drawing all of this out to scale on graph paper before planning alterations. You will need to mark lines of vision to and from items you wish to see – for example, an arbour glimpsed from a window. As you do this, a series of lines will emerge, which need not be confined within the garden, for you should consider and include all the things which you like to glimpse outside. From all this you can establish what you wish to be the major focal point and determine where hard surfaces, in the way of paths, steps and paved areas, are required to interconnect the viewpoints. Remember that even a relatively small garden can be made to seem much larger than it is by blocking parts of views and looping paths around. Plotting what you want to see also identifies what you want to obscure and which areas will need to be planted out with camouflaging evergreens or obscured by a wall, hedge or fence.

Ground planning, more than any other process, will determine the style of your garden and whether it is to be formal or informal. Sometimes the site dictates style, but with careful planning and much ingenuity a formal garden with straight lines can be successfully contrived on an irregular site or a garden with serpentine walks on a flat, rectangular one.

Ground planning is also crucial in maintenance terms, for all that is not a hard surface, being grass, shrubbery, flower or vegetable bed, will require regular cultivation. So when you have achieved your initial layout, make sure it fits your horticultural ambitions and commitment. You can then plot the planting, keeping in mind the need to establish the garden's basic pattern, an arrangement of lines and shapes which, because of their proportions, will give you pleasure for the whole year.

PATHS & PAVING

*P*aths and areas of paving can give a garden as much style and character as the plants. They extend architecture, with all the durable qualities of building materials, into the garden and in this way link the house with the world of nature. They also provide contrasting textures that enhance the appearance of plants: for instance feathery foliage always looks lighter and more delicate beside paving than it does when seen against grass, and a brick path will neatly define the edge of a lawn.

Paths are the very bones of the garden, the framework on which it is built. They divide the garden into different areas, defining the spaces available for planting and linking them together. They play a practical role in the maintenance of the garden, of course, providing easy access to beds at all seasons of the year and allowing equipment such as wheelbarrows to be moved about the garden. But they are, first and foremost, the means whereby the garden is displayed. A walk along a well-designed garden path can present a series of pleasurable experiences: going past flowers, shrubs and trees which are themselves delightful, you are lured on by arches, pergolas and arcades in the direction of such features as sundials, statues, fountains and gazebos. The path establishes mood and style, whether it is straight and formal or winding and informal. By narrowing a path in false perspective or by the clever positioning of flanking plants, paths can even give a small garden the appearance of being larger than it is.

A paved surface directly outside the house makes an attractive area for welcoming and entertaining, for eating and sitting out. And it can

This central path of weathered yellow brick is plain and simple – and therein lies its appeal. It never dominates in terms of colour, texture or pattern nor does it compete for attention with the flowers and foliage. Its long undulating lines indicate movement and lead the visitor on through the wonderfully coloured borders of soft blues and greens, white and pale purple. The lime-green flowers of lady's mantle (*Alchemilla mollis*) spilling out at regular intervals along the pathway give the garden a loose, informal structure.

1

1 A small paved garden can be remarkably successful, especially if, as here, it is softened by abundant planting, and it has none of the problems associated with caring for a lawn. The square central pool holds the composition together, and there is a refreshing contrast between the shimmering water and the hardness of the paving. The stone and the pale brick path leading to it may have looked rather hard at first, but they have both weathered attractively.

2 The paving materials and planting in this distinctly modern garden make an interesting comparison with those in the more traditional one opposite. Here, the chequerboard of concrete slabs with pebble-filled runnels creates a very regular, hard-looking texture and is ideally suited to the bold leaf shapes, particularly the feathery spikes of bamboo.

be extended to prove that it is perfectly possible to have a successful and stunning garden without including a lawn in the design.

Paths fall neatly into two categories: those which are main arteries and must be wide enough to walk along two abreast, and narrow subsidiary ones which enable access for weeding. When planning paths and paving you must combine functional requirements with a scheme that will enhance the design of the garden. Bearing this in mind, it is sensible to mark on a ground plan all the features which need access by way of a hard surface: the house doors, gates, garage, out-buildings, and so on. It is also useful to consider which need to be reached easily and which are merely utilitarian and can be screened. A straight path leading to an ugly back gate is no adornment, whereas if the path changes course the gate can be hidden.

Once such basics are known, they need to be incorporated into a pattern of paths and paved areas which contribute to the delight of the garden, are fundamental to its layout and structure and integral to the enjoyment of its planting.

The materials to choose for paths and paved areas will depend on the existing architecture, of garden buildings as well as of the house, on the formality or otherwise of the garden scheme and on the amount of traffic which a surface will carry. And, of course, the over-riding factor will be the limits of your budget; if this is low, a satisfactory short-term solution could be to combine a good-quality material, such as stone, with a material such as gravel that is cheaper. When funds are available the paving can be upgraded. Combinations are not always a matter of compromise. Sometimes new man-made materials look good used in conjunction with a modest amount of traditional paving. Imitation stone, for example, married to genuine old brick can be extremely effective.

The range that is commercially available from builders' yards and garden centres can be limiting, too. Take your time about choosing the material, and certainly do not buy in quantity on the spur of the moment. It is a good idea to collect small samples of paving, both traditional and man-made, to see what they look like in your own garden. Consider their texture and whether they can be used to make an interesting pattern, either alone or combined with another material. Examine the effects of light and rain on the materials and the way they complement plants. Paving should never dominate the plants it is designed to enhance – which is why hectic red and yellow concrete slabs should be avoided at all costs. Choose materials that will mellow. Think about the safety aspect, too: does the material get slippery when wet?

Stone is the most beautiful of all materials, and it will be particularly appropriate if it is local. It is often ruled out on the grounds of prohibitive cost, but a little stone, however expensive, used in conjunction with a cheaper material, may be well worth the indulgence. However, very acceptable reconstituted stone slabs, made from crushed stone, are available commercially and, if the surface is rough, will weather attractively. To pave with granite setts is almost as expensive as to use stone but, if you are lucky enough to have access to a supply of setts and can afford them, they make delightful paths and paved areas, especially when *2*

2

3

they are arranged carefully in geometric patterns.

Bricks, especially old ones, make lovely paths and they can be laid in innumerable patterns, herringbone and basket-weave among them. Bricks come in a variety of colours: red, grey-black and yellow. Care must be taken that none of these is too dark or garish in tone; ideally, they should match the brick of the architecture. Make sure, however, that bricks are frost-resistant, otherwise they will crumble in time. Quarry tiles have the same rusty tones as some bricks, although they are smoother textured. They are particularly appropriate for use in a small courtyard garden or for a terrace area near the house.

Cobbles and pebbles are not comfortable to walk on but they can be laid in wet cement to form very beautiful patterns. The best way to use them is as a decorative element in a paving scheme of another material. This is a useful way to use gravel, too, although it does make a handsome path in its own right. It is not really suitable for areas near house doors, but if laid on a good foundation it can make a classic garden path that is easy to keep weed-free with herbicides and can be tidied extremely easily with an occasional raking.

1 An extremely stylish small garden that is very contemporary in feel. It makes use of contrasting materials – tiling and wood decking – and changes of level, cleverly combined with a sheet of water. Its absolute precision – the elegant proportions of each area contained within straight lines and sharp corners – suggests that this is an architect-designed garden. In the raised beds, which are important features of the garden, great use has been made of varied leaf shapes – flowers are confined to the pool. Notice how the reflective qualities of the water are essential to the success of this tiny garden.
2 A delightful rustic path winds its way down through a planting of primroses and hostas. It is paved with sections of tree trunk – an appropriate material for the less formal parts of the garden away from the house, although it does get dangerously slippery when wet.
3 The appeal of old railway sleepers is that they weather so attractively. They give this private little hedged garden a mellow feel, set amongst gravel in a regular pattern and used for paths, as a seat and to edge a raised bed containing herbs. Sleepers are no longer cheap to buy and can be difficult to find.

1

2

The variety of cement slabs and bricks is very large and great care must be taken over choice. Stick to neutral colours – pale beige, buff, stone – and even then be cautious and never be taken in by the names, such as 'genuine York paving', that they are sold under. Be warned, you could end up with something really awful. Using the slabs in conjunction with other materials tends to give more interesting results than bland areas of concrete.

Wood can be used as a hard surface but does decay and is also slippery when wet. Nevertheless, it can look striking, generally when used informally – for example, sections of tree trunk sunk as stepping stones or railway sleepers massed as a terrace. Wood decking is another possibility, particularly contrasted with other materials.

Once you have selected the materials you can draw a scaled plan of all the paved areas and paths, slab by slab or brick by brick, drawing in all the patterns and marking apertures left for plants. You will then be able to work out exactly how much of each material you will require.

The main paved area in any garden is usually close to the house. Because there will be a lot of wear and tear, it must be of durable materials. The slippery surface of wood or uneven cobbles or gravel that might be trampled through the house are obviously all unsuitable. What is demanded is a virtually flat surface of brick, stone or concrete slabs, or a mixture of these, arranged in an interesting pattern and allowing beds for plants, including ones next to the wall of the house for climbers. Even if it is a service area, its treatment need never be prosaic, a deadening sea of concrete slabs.

If you have only a very small garden there is much to be said in favour of paving all areas except where you want spaces for trees, shrubs and flowers. On the whole, this is a far more satisfactory treatment of a small site than the pocket handkerchief lawn, which will not stand up well to wear. This is also a happy solution where the soil is poor; new soil need be brought in only for the beds. With lavish planting and the addition of containers, a paved garden can be really elegant. Of course, the

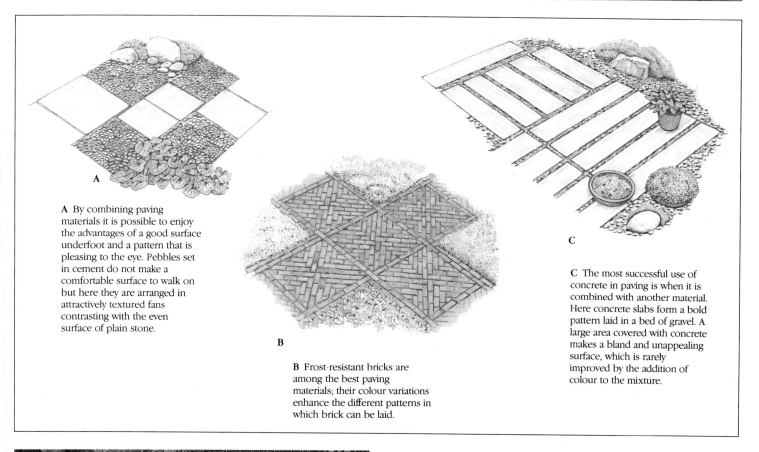

A By combining paving materials it is possible to enjoy the advantages of a good surface underfoot and a pattern that is pleasing to the eye. Pebbles set in cement do not make a comfortable surface to walk on but here they are arranged in attractively textured fans contrasting with the even surface of plain stone.

B Frost-resistant bricks are among the best paving materials; their colour variations enhance the different patterns in which brick can be laid.

C The most successful use of concrete in paving is when it is combined with another material. Here concrete slabs form a bold pattern laid in a bed of gravel. A large area covered with concrete makes a bland and unappealing surface, which is rarely improved by the addition of colour to the mixture.

1 In this formal garden of great simplicity and perfect symmetry all interest focuses on the paving. Four paths made of small rectangular granite setts and edged with trained ivy lead to the centrepoint, a spiralling circle. The narrowness of the setts and their soft tones help to create a pattern of great delicacy.

2 Wonderful paved areas can be made by combining a variety of materials and laying them in inventive patterns. Here, a square flagstone set into a diamond of tiles, laid on edge, surrounded by dark bricks, forms a central motif on an octagonal platform paved with stone flags and also outlined in brick. Note how the precise geometry of the bricks is counterbalanced by the irregular shapes of the flags and tiles.

3 Repetition of pattern also produces interesting paths. This one flanked by beds of bearded irises consists of a combination of square granite setts arranged in a chain of diamonds and loose gravel. There are numerous variants of this, using the same or different materials and other geometric shapes.

paved areas must be interesting to look at, not all of the same material but a mixture which combines different textures, colours and patterns in the arrangement. A word of caution, though: avoid using too many materials in a small space – two or, at the most, three will be sufficient; any more and the effect will be unnecessarily fussy.

Paths and paved areas can sometimes benefit from edging, which gives them an additional, decorative, emphasis. Old Victorian tile edging, often with a rope finish, is beautiful and is now available in reproduction. An equally good edging can be devised with brick, laid either diagonally or upright, perhaps arranged to form a low crenellated boundary. Other forms of edging can now be obtained in reconstituted stone, which is also attractive for a formal path. Only make use of edging if you really wish to outline a pathway or flowerbed. Even then you should always allow some plants to flop over, concealing sections of the edging, otherwise the effect will be excessively hard and unsympathetic.

A selection of plants suitable for growing in paving is given in List 1 on page 138.

1 Gravel remains a classic material for paths, and is one of the simplest and the cheapest of all. It suits formal and informal gardens alike. It is used to considerable effect here on a path that meanders its way through an interesting collection of herbaceous plants. With appropriate edging, it would look equally at home in a more formal setting.

2 Stone slabs cut and laid on the diagonal are an imaginative, yet simple, paving material. When combined with a sprawling, self-seeding carpet of cowslips lightly flecked with forget-me-nots they make a path quite out of the ordinary. The plants growing in the cracks between slabs add to its charm.

3 There is no reason why paths in vegetable patches should not be as interesting as those elsewhere in the garden. And imposing a geometric structure on the vegetable garden by means of paths can make it into a decorative potager. This has been done here by laying paths of granite setts to varying widths – three-setts wide for main arteries, narrower for those used primarily as access for weeding and the harvesting of crops – and creating unusually shaped beds, like this delightful triangular tomato bed.

2

3

STEPS

*T*he use of steps in the landscaping of a garden was invented by the Renaissance architect Bramante (1444–1514) in executing a commission for Pope Julius II. Bramante used grand staircases, balustrading and gentle ramps to connect terraces and emphasize level changes in a scheme linking the Vatican with the Villa Belvedere on the hillside behind it. The result was magnificent and hugely influential, the first of the great architectural gardens, which was copied and adapted for centuries afterwards.

As Bramante demonstrated with such skill, steps are an architectural device that evokes a fundamental human response. Not only do we find them interesting to look at and to experience but they create expectations. The most elementary example is going up a slight hill to enjoy a view; walking up the sweeping staircase of the Belvedere is, perhaps, the most sophisticated version of the same impulse. There is no doubt that steps add drama. The fact that steps are so firmly associated with 'making an entrance' tells us a great deal.

Changes of level can be the result of necessity, because the site actually slopes down or up to the house, or of deliberate manufacture, because a ground plan which is totally flat is just dull and lacking in the sparkle that a single step up or down can give it. Be cautious, however, for dramatic changes in level will almost certainly be exceedingly expensive to achieve however you effect them.

There is a fine balance between nature and artifice to be observed. Within the space of a small garden more than one or two changes of level are likely to look over-contrived, although there are two places

Steps and the changes of level they bring add enormously to the
success of any garden. This flight curves up a slope by
way of two landings, from where you can stop and look
back, and then disappears between ivy-covered brick walls.
The wide slabs of stone used for the tread project over the
brick risers, giving a strong horizontal shadow which
is in happy contrast with the undulating shapes of the plants;
these include bergenias, fuchsias and ferns.

within any garden where a change can safely be introduced and not look artificial. The first is where the paved area surrounding the house gives way to the garden proper, the second lies in the middle distance where it can be used as a device of division, particularly in a narrow garden which can seem much wider by the introduction of one or more carefully placed steps. Such changes in level would be interesting to contemplate, either from or looking towards the house.

Steps near the house should relate to its architecture and building materials and, therefore, are usually formal. The further away the steps are from the house the less formal they need be, but they should be in harmony with the linking paths. The materials for both are the same (see pages 13–16).

Steps have to be tackled at the ground plan stage. Start by drawing their position on the plan, deciding how many, how wide and their style. The general consensus seems to be that the tread should be between 12 and 18 inches (30 and 45 centimetres) and the rise between 4 and 6 inches (10 and 15 centimetres). Make them generous; it is a common fault to make steps too small and apologetic as though the garden were visited only by dwarfs and gnomes instead of human beings.

In style and construction, steps can be as simple as railway sleepers or logs embedded in a slope with bark chippings as treads. They can be plain turf steps, romantic but slippery if wet. They can be as elaborate as an architect-designed double flight of stone with a landing and balustrading.

Unless you are extremely accomplished, the construction of formal flights will require the services of a builder. For the best results, you will need to prepare specifications, including a ground plan and picture references of what you want, and exact details of flanking walls, piers, coping and other embellishments. When you are assembling this material, it is worth turning to the architectural section of the local public library for inspiration. Be adventurous. The design of garden steps has largely got stuck in the era of Gertrude Jekyll and Sir Edwin Lutyens; watered-down versions of these Edwardian classics have become clichés.

Most flights of steps in a small garden will be modest in number, perhaps just one step indicating a change of mood, in terms of design and planting, from one part of a garden to another. For example, a few formal steps might lead from a pergola into a flower garden, from where an

A A good solution to a modest change of level in a garden can be a short flight of conventional squared steps.

B In a more imaginative treatment the steps might be built with their corners cut across and the top level of the flight spanned by an arch.

C In another elaborate variation the front of the steps could swell out in a curve. The steps are given added importance by the way the hedge is clipped.

informal flight made of wooden risers and gravel might lead into a shrubbery. By their materials, steps can anticipate what is to come.

Steps can also add importance to a focal point such as a summerhouse, sundial or statue. A garden that is all paving, however varied that may be in pattern and texture, also benefits from at least one change of level. There is no doubt that steps respond dramatically to the fall of light, providing strong alternating light and dark areas in parallel lines which present a sharp contrast with undulating leaf shapes.

Major flights of steps to accommodate a steep slope present more complex problems. A long straight flight in a small garden is an undesirable feature. It would be far better to break the steps

The original of these classic steps, three projecting semi-circles running counterpoint to two recessed ones, was illustrated in Serlio's *Architettura*, a famous Renaissance work published in 1544. The pretty planting of campanula in the crevices emphasizes the *chiaroscuro* effect, light against dark.

with a landing or terrace half way down and then continue either with a wider single flight or, even better, with a double one that extends in opposite directions. A curved horseshoe flight of steps is another possibility on a steepish slope, and it can look particularly handsome in a formal garden setting. Where a flight parts or curves, an ideal site for the location of a garden ornament will be created, particularly for something classical.

Steps can be elaborated in a number of ways. They can be emphasized by the addition of a pair of flanking urns, pineapples or even statues. If they are generous enough, there can be pots on every step, although terracotta ones are subject to damage by frost and might have to be taken in during the winter months. Attention can also be drawn to the steps by planting trees of naturally formal shape at each side of the bottom step.

Be cautious about plants actually on or at the side of the steps. They can cause slips and falls, and a wary eye must be kept on their encroachment. Informal steps with plenty of space can take plants in the crevices. Formal steps, however, should be kept formal – that is their charm – and their architecture should not be cluttered up and obscured by unnecessary foliage and flowers.

It is true to say that the basic safety measures generally adhered to within the house are promptly ignored by so many when it comes to the garden. Steps can be a very real hazard. Bearing this in

1

2

3

1 This gentle ascent of granite curbing combines attractively with bricks, and offers a rugged contrast to the long, feathery grasses that border the steps.
2 An extremely ingenious flight of brick steps laid in a basket-weave pattern incorporates a centre slope, an idea that could be adapted to take wheeled traffic. I would have placed a pair of turquoise plant containers on the corners of the parapets, rather than just one.
3 A lovely informal staircase made of logs that have been embedded into the ground as risers with wide grass treads. The wood has split and weathered beautifully; the grass, though, must be cut by hand.
4 Three steps, flanked by urns and overhung by a laburnum, lead up to a paved circular platform. It is a very theatrical introduction to the upper level.

4

This contemporary house spills out into its garden in a most appealing manner. It is a perfect example of the merging of house and garden, the one flowing naturally into the other. Its casual appearance, however, is deceptive for the garden is clearly professionally designed. The steps are constructed of seasoned heavy timber planking and concrete and planted with prostrate cotoneasters. These are the kind of very sociable steps that make natural seats.

mind, serious consideration should always be given to adding balustrading, handrails or some other form of support to any flight of steps. Of course, not everyone can afford parapet walls or imitation stone balustrading but a wooden hand-rail should be within reach of most pockets. Do not, however, negate the purpose of a balustrade or handrail by entwining it with a climber, such as a rambler rose, which pricks the hand.

Plants suitable for growing on and around steps are given in Lists 1 and 5 on pages 138–9.

ENCLOSURE, DIVISION & ENTRY

Gardening begins with the notion of enclosure, division and entry. The concept of a garden is a piece of land that is treated differently from what lies outside its bounds. That is what sets it apart from uncultivated wild nature and makes it such an expression of personal taste and style. And what actually sets it apart physically is its boundaries, in the form of walls, fences, hedges and gates. They must be crossed before admission is granted into what is perceived as a purely private world.

Enclosures within a garden play a vital structural role in the composition. Hidcote, in the Cotswold hills, provides a superb example of their effective use. Here a bare hillside has been transformed by hedges of yew and hornbeam into a series of corridors and rooms, each containing a theme, such as the red garden, and each also carefully orchestrated in terms of entrances and exits to frame vistas and views, enticing the visitor on to further delights.

Making any kind of enclosure is an exciting adventure – from plotting it on a plan to choosing the materials, determining its shape and whether it should be transparent or solid. This is precisely the way all gardens over the centuries have begun. Decisions are based on what area needs to be enclosed, whether views are enjoyable or unsightly as well as the necessity of establishing shelter and protection from wind, cold and frost. The height of the enclosure, and the amount of sun and shade in the garden, will be determined by the direction the land faces and the level of privacy the gardener wants to achieve.

Walls, fences and hedges perform virtually the same functions, but present a variety of choices in terms of budget, time span and style. A hedge is clearly a long-term investment, a fence an immediate and cheap solution. A herbaceous border will be set off to perfection against the closely knit green velvet pile of a yew hedge. An open-work fence in an interesting pattern will support plants but also allow peeping from one area into another in anticipation. An arch dripping with roses may be just the thing to frame a distant focal point.

It is sensible to plan from the outside walls and work inwards, deciding where, for instance, a hedge should be allowed to grow high to secure protection or to obscure an ugly view, or where a gate might be better positioned for access. Then slowly move inwards, planning the screening of necessities that are rarely ever beautiful to look at: garages, toolsheds, oil tanks and dustbins. That done, you will be left with the area that is to be the garden proper. And if it is large enough, it could be sub-divided into more than one space by the introduction of a hedge or screen.

It is these features – walls, hedges, fences and gates – which, with trees, provide the key vertical elements in a garden's composition. They are, above all, architecture and, as with all architecture, good proportion is of the utmost importance. The house must be the first point of reference, for house and garden must form a single entity. Just as important is the human scale in determining the appropriate height of arches, gates and hedges and in establishing what can and cannot be seen over.

These elements are the garden's skeleton. They must be interesting in material, colour and shape. Give them careful thought – hasty decisions may later be regretted.

WALLS

Walls are as old as the art of gardening itself and an essential part of its repertory over thousands of years. I have always loved the romance of the medieval walled garden, the *hortus conclusus*, with its solid castle-like crenellated walls. The wall was used as protection from the outside world, as a defence against the wind and as a support for beautiful climbers and espaliered fruit trees. We can still learn much from the walled gardens of the past.

By their very nature, walls introduce a sense of order into a garden. They vary in their architectural content, some being punctuated by doors and windows, some being stretches of plain unadorned surface. Free-standing walls and the walls of houses and out-buildings almost certainly relate to openings for access doors, gates and arches; these, in turn, connect with the paths that lead to them. Within the garden itself there can be lesser retaining walls, ones which control rises and falls in the terrain and are also linked with paths and steps. The fact that all these features are interconnected makes a vital point: that the materials from which they are constructed must harmonize, leading the eye gently on from one to another.

Natural stone is the most sympathetic of all materials for plants. It weathers beautifully and readily grows the lichen and moss that add so enormously to its attractiveness. But a stone wall is very costly. Flint, rose-red and pale yellow brick walls are equally sensitive plant partners. Small old rose-red bricks are by far the best, whereas bricks mass-produced from the Victorian era can be jarring in colour and texture. These can, however, be transformed by careful planting. By

A rough and weathered stone wall, its uneven surface responding to the play of light, is softened by moss and lichen and the ferns and other plants growing in its crevices. *Cotoneaster horizontalis* may have been planted in the wall, but it is more likely to be self sown. It is a deciduous shrub with surface-hugging herringbone growth, and carries heavy crops of brilliant red berries in late summer; in addition, the leaves turn a good colour before falling. A stone wall such as this one needs plenty of plant life if it is not to look bald.

1

far the least attractive material is concrete but even that can be rendered and painted. Whatever material the wall is made of, it is important to remember that it will require regular maintenance to avoid the effects of rising damp, to ensure the pointing is in good order and foundations are not undermined by tree roots.

The front of a house is usually its design showpiece so be very cautious about clothing it with climbers. In the case of the sides and, above all, the back, where many small gardens are situated, planting invariably comes to the rescue, covering or camouflaging architectural blemishes from soil pipes to ugly fenestration. I always find it surprising how little attention is paid to concealing outbuildings, such as garages and sheds, which are often constructed of ugly materials. They can easily be screened, either by hedges or climbers. Naturally, what can be grown will be affected by the

1 A wall of stone and brick strikingly clothed with a climbing rose. Although they can look gaunt in the winter, roses, especially repeat-flowering varieties, are good for planting against walls. Even some of the shrub roses can be trained successfully, including 'Réveil Dijonnais', which is in full flower here. Its strong colour, scarlet-crimson with yellow centre, means that its companions should be chosen with care.
2 There are almost as many good plants that prefer or tolerate shade as there are those that demand full sun. Ferns are an obvious example. The firethorns (*Pyracantha*), trained around the window, are spiky evergreens that are vigorous growers even in shady positions. They have white flowers in early summer but it is for their bright berries that these shrubs are particularly valued. Another shade-tolerant plant, the yellow-flowering *Jasminum nudiflorum*, would give this wall colour even in winter.

2

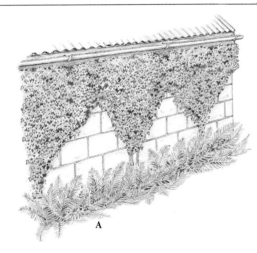

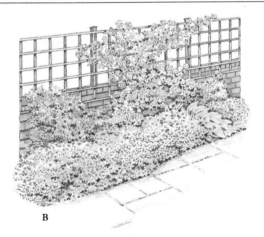

A Gardeners frequently inherit features that are best concealed by skilful planting of climbers, such as varieties of ivy (*Hedera*).

B The cheapest way to extend a low wall is by adding sections of trellis. The climbers they support can create an effective screen.

C Brick is an outstandingly versatile material, when laid imaginatively, giving interesting patterns to walls and paving.

direction the house or out-building faces and by the height of the walls. On the whole, walls are a gardener's ally, guarding against the elements and retaining the warmth of the sun. Remember, however, that the soil at the base of walls is often dry and difficult.

But before you get to the planting stage consider whether painting the wall or attaching trellis would improve its overall appearance. Painting the wall white or a shade of off-white can provide an attractive background to climbers and lighten the whole aspect of the garden. If the stucco or brick is painted, you must select suitable climbers that can be pulled away from the surface to allow for repainting. However, it may be more sensible not to paint it at all.

That said, not to plant up at least one wall of the house is to lose valuable space. Such planting provides a vital link between house and garden – especially important in a small garden where you rarely lose sight of the house.

Planting climbers on a house wall brings a bonus for those indoors. The texture of foliage and the colour and scent of flowers can provide year-round satisfaction, starting with the bright yellow flowers of the winter-flowering jasmine, moving through the japonicas (*Chaenomeles*) in spring to the abundance of summer roses and clematis, and

1 The boulders in this wall contain an enormous variety of shapes and colours, including greys, silvers and browns. The wall is a bold and informal feature which suits the strongly coloured planting.
2 Ribbing gives this concrete wall interesting texture and lessens the somewhat brutal appearance of the material. Concrete should be used sparingly in a small garden otherwise the effect can be municipal and it must always be softened with planting. The two fine shrubs are in spring flower, a cotoneaster in the foreground with the gorgeous tiers of white viburnum blossom behind. The latter is an ideal shrub if you require a 'waterfall' of foliage.
3 A retaining wall of concrete with pebbles embedded and arranged in herringbone-like stripes supports a dramatic Mediterranean planting of a spiky agave, yuccas, rosemary and silver-leaved foliage plants growing amidst a tangle of pink pelargoniums.

1

ending in the autumn with the bright berries of the evergreen pyracantha and cotoneaster and the glow of vine leaves changing from the palest yellow to blood red.

It is a fortunate gardener indeed who inherits or acquires a walled garden. It is a major horticultural and design asset which calls for celebration, not total concealment. But a word of caution if you are considering building from scratch; a proper wooden fence, which will cost less, is better than a poorly built wall of ugly materials.

Ideally, an enclosing garden wall should be at least 6 feet (2 metres) high to ensure privacy and, at the same time, to allow plants to attain their full potential. A low wall can be heightened simply by adding trellis or, if it is finished off with a flat coping, it can be given extra height with containers filled with ivies, and other trailing plants.

Changes of ground level call for low retaining walls, which can look very attractive with a plant spilling over the edge. A 'wall garden' consisting of large stones and boulders will take the sort of cascading plants that suit rock gardens.

The many plants to grow on and against walls differ enormously in their vigour, foliage characteristics, flower colour and seasonal patterns. Climbers and wall shrubs divide themselves into those that thrive best with sun and warmth and those to whom shade is no enemy. You can choose to adorn your walls either formally – for example, with espaliered fruit trees – or informally with a clematis or a honeysuckle.

When choosing plants, bear in mind the colour of the woodwork of the house and that dark walls call for light blooms. Include both evergreens and deciduous plants for all-round interest, and remember that a variety of sizes and shapes of leaf and of flower form will be more interesting visually. Think, too, of the possibilities of encouraging a clematis to twine through another climber, such as through a rose or a wisteria.

My own favourites include yellow-flowered roses such as 'Gloire de Dijon', varieties of clematis and the deciduous self-clinging *Hydrangea petiolaris*. I am also particularly fond of trained fruit trees such as pears, apples and figs, and vines (species of *Vitis*), especially *V. coignetiae*, with huge leaves that colour gorgeously in autumn.

Plants suitable for growing against or on walls are given in Lists 2–5, 12 and 13 on pages 138–41.

1 This extraordinary garden tableau has an effect reminiscent of the most romantic of old country churchyards. Slabs of grey stone have been driven into the ground to form a low dividing wall, its jagged form and hard texture contrasting with the feathery leaves of the ferns, the undulating light and mid-green tones of the hostas and the thin spiky grasses.

2 This inventive wall of cut logs stacked high between solid retaining posts may not be such a long-lasting feature but it certainly makes an unusual and highly imaginative temporary barrier. The beautiful textural combination of the bark and saw marks, the considerable variety in colouring, and the triangular shape of the log ends is quite lovely.

FENCES

*T*he fence was one of the earliest means of dividing wild from cultivated nature and, hence, has been a major ingredient of the garden for centuries. Even in the eighteenth century, when the English landscape style swept away the fences of the old formal gardens all over Europe, a large garden could still be delineated with a delicate fence wending its way over acres, guiding the visitor from temple to statue to grotto to vista. Renaissance gardens were, without exception, defined by elegant palings marking out the domain, the walks and terraces. These were painted in all the colours of the rainbow, often marbled and even adorned with gilding. Sometimes the main posts to a fence would bear a figure clasping an heraldic banner. At the very least, there would be a ball or pineapple. The colour and exotic ornamentation makes our own use of the fence seem very drab in comparison.

We only have to look at engravings or pictures of these fences in the old garden books to realize how enormously varied they were; there was every conceivable style from Gothic through to classical, and including Chinese during the eighteenth century. These illustrations are a mine of ideas for even the smallest garden, for their scale is often extremely modest and domestic.

Fences, like hedges and walls, create enclosure and division. Indeed, they are the only truly 'instant' solution. They have the additional advantage of being relatively cheap. Fences can totally conceal a garden or give tantalizing glimpses of it through fretwork. They can also be used purely in their own right as garden decoration.

A simple series of tall wooden palings with well-finished newel posts provides a handsome boundary to a paved area used as a terrace. The fence's straight lines contrast with the luxuriant planting, which includes good foliage plants as well as flowering perennials. The palings are quite closely spaced but enough of the foliage beyond shows through for garden and woodland to seem related. Notice the off-centre siting of the sundial, with gilding that catches the sunlight.

Fences can be temporary: the simplest wattle fence supported between sturdy posts can provide several years of protection while a hedge grows – bamboo matting can be used to striking effect for the same purpose – turning the fact that the hedge has not yet grown into a visual advantage.

A fence should be approached with the spirit of adventure. Too often, it is treated as a drear necessity. Few things are more dispiriting than the average garden fence, a series of matchboards with terminal posts at intervals caging in a rectangle of earth. Such a fence is rarely high enough to thwart the curious and secure privacy. It is really hardly

1

1 A superb example of the metalwork fence in a design dating from the early nineteenth century. Sadly, the expense and poor quality of design of much modern metalwork make its use for fencing less and less common. The white lattice-work railings form an elegant serpentine; the pattern is continued in the spandrels of the portico and has been repeated in the trellis against the wall of the house. The tumbling growth of self-seeding *Corydalis lutea* softens the lines of the design.
2 A picket fence and gate painted in contrasting colours are set amidst the simplicity of brick path, mown grass, clipped box and flowering trees. This is a classic example, best known from the American colonial tradition which has been re-created at Williamsburg, Virginia.

2

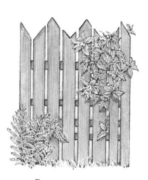

A The finish of a picket fence needs to harmonize with the architecture of the house it surrounds but it can help to give a garden its distinctive character.

B Planting to soften the base or outline of a picket fence must be controlled to allow easy maintenance and also give the garden a mature look.

C Tall iron railings make a handsome boundary to a garden but need to be custom made and, therefore, are always excessively expensive.

D At all seasons of the year the highly decorative outline of this fence will make an extremely attractive boundary or division within the garden.

surprising that, faced with such a depressing boundary, the gardens within them tend to be uninteresting and apologetic – planted in the pretence that the fence does not exist, whereas it remains a deadening unobliterated feature.

The fence should be exactly the opposite, an adornment to the garden, a fitting architectural structure which will show off, to best advantage, the plants growing in front or climbing over it in pretty profusion. As well as defining the boundaries and controlling space, a fence can create surprise and illusion. And, in the case of a solid fence, it will protect both house and plants from cold and wind. Its purpose determines height and style and whether it need be solid or open work.

A house and a small garden are too close in proximity for a fence to be in a style completely at variance. A cottage demands rustic fencing in rough unfinished materials; a nineteenth-century town house calls for formal railings at the front. A modernist house would suit bold straight lines. So before you decide on a fence, look hard at your house for it should at least tell you what will and will not be appropriate to it. The house may have some distinguishing shapes which could be echoed in the fencing design: crenellation, an ogee or Gothic arch, for instance, which could be repeated along the top of a fence, or a diamond-shaped leaded window, which could find repetition in an open lattice-work fence around a little herb or vegetable garden.

When a fence is being used for concealment, to hide dustbins, and so on, solid wooden fencing is the ideal, with climbers, such as jasmine, a vine or a repeat-flowering rose, encouraged to ramble over it. It is far more interesting, however, to develop the

1 Bamboo fencing makes an attractive temporary screen, providing privacy or perhaps blocking an ugly view until the yew hedge that has been planted behind the seat forms an adequate barrier – which may take another four or five years.
2 This screening fence was stark and uninteresting before it was hung with pots of trailing greenery and brightened with containers of busy lizzies (*Impatiens*).

2

use of wooden fencing as a means of defining areas within the garden itself. A prettily designed low fence can delineate a terrace, flank a wall or enclose a flowerbed. Its architectural qualities give definition to an area, and details such as decorative profiling, lattice-work and finials give year-round delight. In addition, the fence can be underplanted or entwined with climbers. Think, for instance, of using such a fence for dividing the flower garden from the area planted with vegetables. If it were high enough, it could be used for a crop of summer runner beans or as a support for a hop or vine or even for espaliered fruit trees.

In the past, wood was an inexpensive form of fencing, but these days properly seasoned timber, whether oak, chestnut or pine, is quite an investment. The cheaper woods are more easily available in ready-made fencing but the designs are often very poor. A visit to the average garden centre or builder's yard quickly reveals how far our standards have fallen in this century. If you want good fencing for your garden there is little alternative but to have it made or, at the least, adapted from some available stock fencing. Most builders' yards ought to contain at least lengths and sections of trellis, wattle, woven slats and split bamboo: all of these are serviceable, particularly if they are to be largely concealed by planting. You may have to go to a timber merchant for dressed or rustic timber from which to construct something more interesting for the fences that occupy a more prominent position in the garden scheme.

Metal can be a very appropriate fencing material, particularly in urban areas. Antique iron railings or good copies in wrought iron or aluminium can be found, but at a premium. The simple classic designs of the past have never been bettered or displaced. In terms of maintenance, they are an enduring investment, requiring only regular painting and freeing from rust. Other forms of fencing hardly contribute to the beauty of the garden, especially of the small garden, where you would never be able to escape the full horrors of them. These include plastic wire-mesh stretched between concrete posts, chicken wire and plastic fencing. Avoid all of them. They are just plain ugly.

The range of colours that fences and railings can be painted is much wider than generally acknowledged. Railings tend to be uniformly painted black or dark green, whereas in the past they were a variety of colours from a very pale green to

1

1 A fence should always have a visual point – but not necessarily a practical one. Here, a low fence of solid wooden stakes has been driven straight into the ground to make a bold border for a bed of delphiniums and catmint (*Nepeta × faassenii*).

2

2 Inspired by the traditions of Japanese gardening, this fence is the simplest of structures. Upright wooden posts support a 'trellis' of bamboo held together by knotted lengths of dark twine, the whole set into gravel. European and American interpretations of Japanese gardens are rarely successful but this adaptation makes an interesting visual divide that allows almost unrestricted view of the garden beyond.

ultramarine blue with touches of gold. In the case of wood, the story is much the same. In hot climates vivid colours – reds, yellows and blues – are used with great success, although in cooler climates they could look absolutely dreadful. On the whole, white and off-white shades together with dark green are the safest – and, undoubtedly, that is the reason why they are most widely used.

The rediscovery of different paint effects could, I think, have potential. Dragged paint, marbling, stipple and rag-roll might be worth an experiment. It may well be, too, that a particularly pretty internal fence which has delightful finials could even take a touch of gilding. Decorating in this extravagant way was quite common before the eighteenth century, although it does require a sure eye to bring it off. This could be particularly effective when a fence is counterbalanced by the rich green of a hedge.

Fences should always, of course, be thought of in conjunction with planting. Indeed, one of the commonest and most emphatic statements is an open-work fence painted white and set against the dark green leaves of yew or *Thuja* or the russet of a hornbeam or beech hedge in winter. Such a picture can be further embroidered with a foreground planting of naturalized bulbs, from early snowdrops to late-flowering narcissi.

Solid fences will take the same planting as walls, but with transparent decorative fences there are opportunities for really imaginative effects, such as contrasting the geometry of the repeating pattern with a climber in the form of a scented rose or a clematis. The effect can even be changed from year to year by planting annuals such as nasturtiums, which burst through in a tangle of orange or yellow bloom, or, if your fence is in the sun, morning glory (*Ipomoea*) with its delightful sky-blue trumpet-shaped flowers.

A final thought: a picket fence and gate at the front of a house are often an opportunity for a spring planting of bulbs – crocuses, daffodils and narcissi – just outside the boundary; the result is a charming seasonal welcome to visitors.

A selection of plants suitable for growing on fences is given in Lists 2–4, 12 and 13 on pages 138–41.

1

1 Well-made timber fencing of good design is a neat finish to this seaside garden, which includes a dense planting of shrubs and large grasses. When choosing plants for exposed coastal gardens like this one, make sure that they will tolerate salt-laden air.

2 A garden within a garden can be defined by walls, hedges or fences. A yew hedge marks the back boundary and the other three sides are enclosed by a trellis fence supported by handsome square posts. Trellis has also been used to form two pyramids suitable for clematis, for instance *C. viticella*, or a rose such as 'Golden Showers'. Trellis fencing of this kind could be painted to make it more dominant or it could be planted with climbers.

3 Variations of the trellis pattern are used in these wooden fences that 'cage in' old-fashioned roses. Many of the old roses are extraordinarily beautiful but they flower only once a year and they can be sprawling untidy growers. These elegant little enclosures are an ingenious way of giving the garden structure and form throughout the year.

2

3

HEDGES

Good hedges are one of the glories of the garden. Until the advent of the landscape style in the eighteenth century, hedges were an essential part of any scheme; by training and fashioning them into geometric patterns, nature was reduced to its proper order. Hedges were grown to form squares, rectangles, circles and other shapes, stretching out from the house in deliberate contrast with the wild undisciplined terrain beyond. That tradition of forming rooms by means of hedges is very much part of this century's garden-making practice. For small-garden makers, it is a tradition certainly worth pursuing. It is far more fruitful to adapt one or two rooms of a large garden to a tiny space than to attempt to reproduce in miniature the elements of a landscape park.

Hedges provide a wonderfully sympathetic background to many smaller plants. Garden ornament, and particularly sculpture, is likewise shown to great advantage set against the green wall of a hedge. Such ornaments will inevitably be sited at the centre of a garden room, or at the close of a vista, nestling in a niche or arch formed by careful training of the hedge.

I tend to measure a garden by its hedges. They reflect so accurately not only the gardener's sense of design but his or her level of commitment. Fences and walls create instant divisions, whereas hedges demand time and regular maintenance. They have other drawbacks, too: they are not as secure, they take up more room and their spreading roots can affect the performance of other plants. Nonetheless, hedges are fine and handsome garden features, living

An elegant tapestry hedge of two varieties of beech, green and copper (*Fagus sylvatica* and *F. s.* 'Purpurea'), gives a dappled harlequin effect. In winter the leaves of both turn a coppery rust but they will not fall until the spring.
The two plants have a similar growth rate, an advantage over a hedge made up of different species – for example, holly, hornbeam, quickthorn and yew – although this would have more varied seasonal changes, ranging from contrasting leaf colours and shapes to bare branches with evergreens.

1

1 Cotton lavender (*Santolina chamaecyparissus*) makes a lovely smoky-grey low hedge. In this sunny garden much has been made of the contrast between its soft colouring and the darker foliage of the plants, including tapering cones of bay (*Laurus nobilis*), that it encloses. Cotton lavender needs to be trimmed regularly throughout the summer not only to preserve its clipped geometry but also to prevent the appearance of its conspicuous yellow flowers, which would radically upset the balance of the garden.
2 Box (*Buxus sempervirens*) is one of the most versatile plants to use for low hedges. It is slow growing but responds well to close trimming and thrives in shade as well as in full sun. The dwarf form *B. s.* 'Suffruticosa' is suitable for use as a low edging. Here a small parterre of castellated box contains a loose planting of winter savory and the handsome blue form of rue (*Ruta graveolens* 'Jackman's Blue').

architecture which divides and organizes the garden space. There is a great art in determining the siting, the height and the shape of hedges. Whether they need to be formal or informal, very high or very low, evergreen or deciduous, will depend very much on the style of the garden and the house. There are other factors that could be involved as well: the need to obliterate an unpleasant view, for example, to disguise a service area, or to establish some sense of privacy.

Without a doubt, hedges are a long-term commitment and so they should be planned from the outset on a ground plan. Plot them, even go to the lengths of drawing them to scale on to card and glueing them into position. It is a good idea to place the model in the centre of the garden on a sunny day and note the shadows cast by the proposed hedges at different times. At this early stage, before any money is spent, it is very important to think

carefully about how the full-grown hedge will affect the rest of the garden design and planting.

The ideal time to plant evergreens is in spring, and deciduous hedges in autumn; containerized stock can be planted at virtually any time. The young plants can be delicate and may need some temporary screening until they become established. The number of plants required will depend on your choice, but it is a sensible plan to order two or three extra in case there are any casualties. However impatient for results you may be, avoid the temptation to use well-developed hedge plants: they will be slow to settle down and will soon be overtaken by vigorous young plants.

Good preparation of the soil will pay ample return in the form of sustained growth, and regular feeding in the following years is essential. When planting outside the main season pay particular attention to watering. Careful pruning and clipping to shape at the appropriate time of the year will prevent the hedge becoming thin and straggly. That early pruning, which is essential to build up a thick bushy growth, should ensure that the hedge is gently sloped outwards down both sides to allow sunlight to get to the base and prevent the hedge from becoming top heavy. Of course, even when your composition is complete the work is not over. It will still require regular clipping and pruning as well as feeding from time to time.

A good formal hedge may take as many as ten to fifteen years to reach perfection. Some are faster

1 The seasonal changes in hedges of deciduous trees such as beech (*Fagus sylvatica*) and hornbeam (*Carpinus betulus*) are spectacular. The colour contrast in this hedge, shown in mid-autumn turning from green to gold, will be particularly striking in winter when viewed against the dark green leaves and red berries of the holly (*Ilex aquifolium*).
2 An extraordinary striped hedge of yew (*Taxus baccata*) with a pillar of variegated holly (an *Ilex* cultivar) running through it. The yew is slow growing but nonetheless is faster than the holly. A similar effect could be achieved by planting buttresses of a golden fastigiate yew (for example, *T. b.* 'Fastigiata Aureomarginata') along a dark green hedge of the common yew.
3 The purple-leaved berberis (*Berberis thunbergii* 'Atropurpurea') makes a good informal hedge with its wonderfully rich reddish-purple foliage that deepens in colour as winter approaches. It can look rather heavy but here the skilful planting of grasses behind it has given an airy effect.

1

2

3

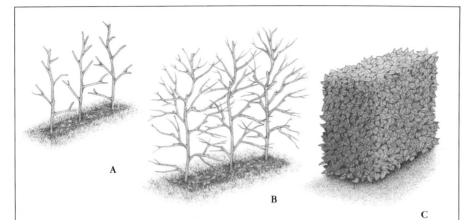

A Plant hedges of beech (*Fagus sylvatica*) and hornbeam (*Carpinus betulus*) between autumn and early spring. Use plants that are about 18 inches (45 cm) high and set them about 18 inches (45 cm) apart. At planting time cut back the main stem and strong side growth by about a third.
B During the second winter cut back the main stem and side growth by about a third once again. This rather severe pruning will take out weak growth and will help to build up a sturdy frame that will be well clothed to the base.
C After the third year begin annual clipping during summer. Shape the hedge to be broader at the base than at the top.

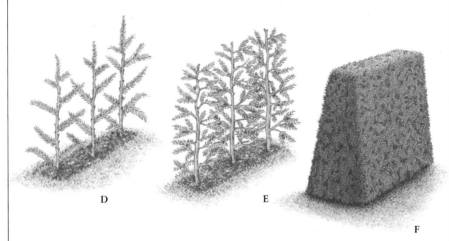

D Yew (*Taxus baccata*), the first choice for hedging, should be planted in well-prepared ground between autumn and early spring, preferably in early spring. Use plants that are about 18 inches (45 cm) high and set them about 22 inches (55 cm) apart. Larger plants are slow to get established. At planting time trim all long and straggly side shoots but leave leaders uncut.
E In the second year begin annual trimming of side growths during summer, ensuring the formation of a hedge with sloping sides.
F Stop the leader when the hedge has reached the required height. An established hedge should only need trimming once annually, in late summer.

growing than others, of course, but even with the fastest you are unlikely to achieve anything resembling a finished effect under five. Watching a hedge grow and shaping it with your own hands is, I believe, one of gardening's great joys. Given today's mechanical aids, the labour commitment is not that large and when the hedge finally reaches maturity and cannot be seen through or over there is a remarkable sense of satisfaction. I must admit that I have always found the first two years after planting quite depressing but, after that, hedges tend to grow rapidly and become more and more interesting. That satisfaction can be had all through those growing years as the hedge is tended and, by judicious clipping and pruning, takes on the shape planned at the drawing-board stage.

Shape is the very essence of a beautiful hedge. At its simplest, a hedge can be cut to a variety of thicknesses and heights; a more complex treatment is to form it into decorative piers, buttresses, arches, windows, crenellations and sweeping curves and curlicues. It is surprising how little attention is paid to the ornamental shape of hedges, for such sculpting adds immeasurably to the visual interest, breaking the monotony of the flat surface and giving full opportunity for a play of light that is comparable to the contrasts of light and shadow on the surface of a building.

The range of plants suitable for large formal hedges is not large. Yew (*Taxus baccata*) is without doubt the queen of hedges and grows far faster than is generally thought, eventually providing a dark green velvety surface which can be readily trained into almost any shape and is the ideal background for every form of garden flower. Box (*Buxus sempervirens*) comes close to it for effect but it is very slow growing indeed; a hedge of any height may take more than a decade to mature. Not quite as slow is holly (*Ilex aquifolium*) with its spiky shiny dark green leaves.

The other evergreens grow faster and some do produce handsome hedges but can never quite compete with yew, box and holly. The best include conifers such as species and hybrids of *Thuja* and *Cupressus*, and Portugal and common laurel (*Prunus lusitanica* and *P. laurocerasus*). The laurels present a maintenance problem for they really ought to be pruned rather than trimmed to avoid scarring the leaves, and the leaves themselves can be too large in scale for a very small garden. Hornbeam (*Carpinus betulus*) and beech (*Fagus sylvatica*) are the deciduous alternatives for formal hedges. Both respond well to clipping and both have the additional virtue of retaining their leaves throughout the winter. These turn a petrified russet brown, and always add greatly to the interest of the garden during its most barren months, an important design consideration.

I have always felt that the tapestry hedge is unjustly neglected. It is made up of intermingled plants, both deciduous and evergreens, such as hornbeam, quickthorn (*Crataegus monogyna*), holly and yew. The effect will be spotty unless you allow at least 1 yard (1 metre) of each variety and do not skimp on the evergreens. The key to a successful tapestry hedge is in using no more than three different plants and balancing colours and leaf sizes. The right combination can be exquisite.

Low-growing formal hedges are used to define the geometric beds of a garden. Indeed, in the case of a box parterre, the garden consists of nothing but hedges; they are usually made of dwarf box (*Buxus sempervirens* 'Suffruticosa') planted in a symmetrical pattern with gravel in between. Technically, this is what is known as a 'closed' parterre in contrast to an 'open' one, which allows for roses or seasonal planting. This type of garden making, based as it is on descriptions of ancient Roman designs, was very fashionable for over two centuries and is still an extremely satisfactory way of dealing with a small space.

The patterns can range from the very complex to a circle imposed on a square or rectangle. Make your design to scale on graph paper and work out the number of plants you will need. The site must be levelled and weed free. For a closed knot, stretch black plastic over the earth and paint the design on top, planting through holes poked in the plastic; cover it with a layer of sand and, finally, of gravel. For an open knot you will need to peg out the site with string to form a grid and inscribe the pattern on the earth itself. Box hedging planted 6 to 8 inches (15 to 20 centimetres) apart will take

The winter sunshine accentuates the transparent quality of this hedge. In summer mature hedges of beech (*Fagus sylvatica*) and hornbeam (*Carpinus betulus*) are thick and dense, but they are thinner in winter, even though the shrivelled coppery leaves do not fall. However, the beauty of the winter foliage more than makes up for the loss of absolute privacy. Beech and hornbeam hedges are both trimmed in midsummer, not in the winter.

1   2

about five years to reach maturity provided it is given regular feeding with bonemeal and annual clipping in early summer.

Nothing quite surpasses dwarf box in a parterre; it has a wonderfully fragrant smell and the pattern can be seen from the moment it is planted. The next best choice is *Santolina chamaecyparissus*, from which a beautiful silvery hedge can be made. Santolina will require replacing every five to eight years and this can easily be done from cuttings taken the previous season. These dwarf hedges give year-long pleasure not only for their own sake but as part of a formal composition. Even in the vegetable garden you might add appropriate edgings to beds for decorative effect – clipped rosemary, for instance, and other herbs may be used but inevitably with a much less formal result.

Informal hedges are a much vaguer category than their formal counterparts. They are composed of shrubs and roses grown in a row to form a loose, and often shamelessly romantic, boundary. The range of plants that can be used is extremely large and what they lack in strict geometric form they more than compensate for with flowers, fragrance and seasonal fruits.

For a tall evergreen hedge, the well-tried laurustinus (*Viburnum tinus*) takes some beating with its shiny evergreen leaves and sweet-smelling white flowers tinged with pink that are such a welcome sight in winter. The smoke tree (*Cotinus coggygria*) is a deciduous alternative. The foliage of the purple-leaved forms is particularly full of interest; it turns yellow, orange and bright crimson before it falls. Rugosa roses make marvellous hedges in even the poorest of soils, giving a fine display of flower over a long period. I am particularly fond of 'Roseraie de l'Haÿ' with its apple-green foliage and its richly scented crimson-purple flowers.

Within the garden there is often a need for low informal hedges around flowerbeds and borders and along paths. Catmint (*Nepeta × faassenii*) brings a poetic haze of soft violet-blue flower heads in summer as well as feathery grey foliage through the growing season. Pinks (*Dianthus*) always look marvellous whatever the variety. And, of course, there is the heady perfume, something that applies equally to rosemary, a plant which should be used far more often for hedging. The upright variety, 'Jessop's Upright', quickly establishes itself as a sturdy hedge with pretty purple flowers in early summer. Rosemary brings fragrance, and so does lavender in all its varieties, making a lovely edging to a summer display of white or yellow roses planted as a bedding scheme.

A selection of plants suitable for hedging and edging is given in Lists 6–8 on pages 139–40.

1 The flame creeper (*Tropaeolum speciosum*) adds a burst of summer colour to a non-flowering hedge. This herbaceous perennial grows from a creeping rhizome and does particularly well in cool moist areas. It would look even better against the dark green of yew.

2 An informal hedge of *Hypericum* 'Hidcote' has a glorious mass of buttercup-yellow flowers during the second half of summer. A hedge with such a strong colour is a very dominant feature and needs careful placing.

3 Camellias are rarely used for hedging but they can be trained to create beautiful informal barriers of glossy dark green leaves and elegant flowers. *Camellia × williamsii* hybrids such as 'St Ewe', which is shown here, are the hardiest. Camellias do not like lime but will thrive in most good acid or neutral soils and will do well even in light shade.

GATES

*T*here is a certain magic about the garden gate. Its seemingly straightforward function of providing access and keeping out unwanted people and stray dogs is loaded with complex psychological overtones. It is the door to another, better, world, always raising the question of what is beyond. The gate is the preface to the garden as a secret and inviolate place to which access has to be granted, as the formidable Miss Mapp of E. F. Benson's hilarious Lucia novels well appreciates: 'When I am here ... I mustn't be disturbed for anything less than a telegram.'

Any gate in a small garden will be important for it will certainly be constantly used and subjected to scrutiny. It is, therefore, a false economy to skimp on it. That lesson we can learn from a visit to any of the great gardens of the past where the first impression is always one of handsome gate piers surmounted by a cornice with a ball, pineapple or heraldic device and supporting wrought-iron gates rich in arabesque pattern and gilding. They make the point in the grand manner that gates are an important element in garden design, whatever the scale on which you are working.

A gate allows passage through a barrier, such as a hedge or solid wall, which usually marks the legal boundaries of the property. For small gardens, the gates will be of two kinds: the entrance gate, often to a small front garden, and the back gate. To these I would add a third, the gate within the garden as a decorative element to create division and surprise.

Its use will determine if the gate should be single or double, solid or transparent, high or low: if the barrier is to secure privacy and shut

A painted picket gate and fence complement this cottage perfectly. They have an unpretentious appeal and in scale, material and design are just right for the straightforward informality – and undeniable charm – of the cottage and the delightfully dishevelled garden surrounding it. A yew hedge with picket gate would have looked equally appropriate from the road, although it might have cast too much shade on the garden. Instead, the conifers add height, privacy and dark colour without dominating.

in animals the gate will need to be solid and high and, if it is to accommodate cars, it will need to be wide – probably a double gate.

The choice of materials will be affected by the use of the gate and by the nature of both the 'wall' it traverses and the house. All three must be in visual accord. In addition, you will need to consider weight – metal, for instance, can be heavy to move – and maintenance implications. Gates are made of wood, metal or plastic, the last being the least attractive due to its synthetic quality. Whatever the choice, it is depressingly true that the range of gates commercially available and of good design is very limited. All too often gates are conceived in terms of basic necessity with no sense of their potential for delight and decoration. Even the simplest

3

1 A solid wooden door set into high brick walls creates total privacy. The door's pointed Gothic style adds to the mystery and heightens the anticipation of what lies beyond the courtyard – or inside the walls. The pink spring foliage of a pieris makes a splash of colour just inside the door.

2 Through the 'transparent' tracery of the wrought-iron Gothic-style gate a herb garden can be glimpsed. Gates like this are difficult to find but you could get one custom made. The dull brick wall has been concealed by clever planting, including a pretty variegated ivy and a large-flowered hybrid clematis that lighten an otherwise dark approach.

3 A simple bamboo gate made in a trellis design combined with a wonderfully ingenious bamboo fence provides an appropriate contrast to the patterns of fan palm leaves and tropical foliage in this oriental garden.

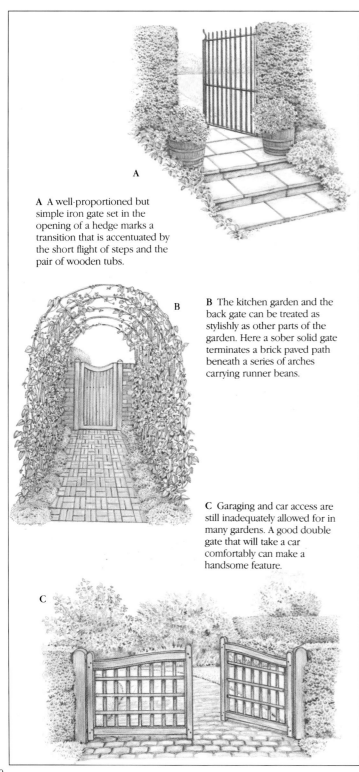

A A well-proportioned but simple iron gate set in the opening of a hedge marks a transition that is accentuated by the short flight of steps and the pair of wooden tubs.

B The kitchen garden and the back gate can be treated as stylishly as other parts of the garden. Here a sober solid gate terminates a brick paved path beneath a series of arches carrying runner beans.

C Garaging and car access are still inadequately allowed for in many gardens. A good double gate that will take a car comfortably can make a handsome feature.

picket gate can be beautifully cut and finished with a plain but elegant handle and hinges.

If you are in the fortunate position of installing new gates or re-siting old ones, you should take the opportunity of looking at the aesthetic as well as the practical factors. Gates literally frame both house and garden, so consider the view through them both ways and how they appear when open and closed. Front gates should be placed to show off the façade of the house to advantage and secure passage to the front door with the minimum of meandering. If possible, internal gates should relate to the view in either direction. Generally, with back gates practical considerations of access, and perhaps security, come first.

Back and side gates are essentially service gates and should be concealed by their placing and by combinations of hedging, fencing, trellis and other forms of screening combined with planting of climbing vegetables, for example, beans or a rampant plant such as Russian vine (*Polygonum baldschuanicum*). Only in rare cases, where the gate leads the eye on to something delectable, such as vistas of open countryside, is there a possibility of turning it to decorative advantage as an integral part of the garden's design.

The front gate is another matter. That is above all architectural, a preface to your house, and it must relate in its scale, design and material to the house to which it leads. The house and your attitude to the world outside will determine whether the aim is to secure privacy by means of a high hedge, walls and solid gate or to present an open approach with low boundary walls, leaving the garden and house open to view and the gate reduced almost to an irrelevance. Planting can enhance both the formality or informality of its appearance: the gate can, for example, be inset into a tangled arch of clematis or into the sharp outline of one of the evergreens, such as yew.

What is neglected and much more interesting is the use of the gate within the garden. The very act of going through a gate from one part of a garden to another gives the illusion of seeing more and produces a sense of anticipation and surprise, whether crossing from pleasure garden to vegetable patch or rose to herb garden. To be effective as a punctuation mark, a gate needs to be placed in a garden of reasonable size. It is particularly appropriate in some of those long rectangular gardens which stretch out with such deadening monotony behind suburban houses. The division of such an area into two by means of a wall, hedge or trellis with a fine arch and gate would immediately achieve a far more satisfactory and attractive disposition of space. Care would need to be taken, however, over the height of the dividing wall to avoid too much shade and, in the case of a hedge, to prevent spreading roots taking nourishment from other plants.

A gate within a garden can also gain further interest if it is approached by one or more steps even in the simplest of paving materials, such as stone, brick or paving slabs. If, on going through a gate, there is a descent, however slight, that too is a pleasurable experience. Such gates are most effective when they allow a glimpse of what lies beyond. In the case of a walled garden a solid wooden door could be very attractive, its opening suddenly revealing the enclosed space.

Not enough attention is paid to the potential of gate piers. All too often they are reduced to a pair of simple square wooden posts. Gate piers, even in a small garden, can be a vehicle for creative ornament, although such elaboration must be in keeping with the overall style of the house and the rest of the garden: a pair of stone eagles with outspread wings would be hardly an appropriate frontispiece to a black and white cottage. Piers are, however, immensely enhanced by the addition of a pair of finials. Balls and pineapples are readily available in reconstituted stone and they lift the effect of the humblest pair of brick piers. Urns are another possibility, giving potential for a full range of seasonal planting from bulbs to pelargoniums. An approach to a garden gate can also be made more important by flanking it at ground level with other types of sculpture – couchant dogs or lions, sphinxes or even a pair of statues – or by a tableau of terracotta pots which can be rearranged and planted according to taste and the time of the year. Finally, any gate can be enhanced by setting it within an arch, whether solid or living.

Gates used in conjunction with fences, hedges and walls can make the divisions within a garden more distinct. Here, a simple white picket gate has been set under an arch in the opening of a high deciduous hedge. The importance of the gate, and of the change from one area of the garden to another, has been emphasized by a symmetrical arrangement of four large terracotta pots containing box pyramids which flank the paved pathway.

ARCHES

*A*garden arch is one of the simplest means which the gardener can use to control how people look at space, since it draws the eye only to what is intended to be seen. It is a framing device, pure and simple. As such, it is one of the oldest and loveliest of all garden features, whether it be solid – that is, made of stone, brick, wood, trellis or metal – or living, the painstaking result of many years of patient training, tying and clipping of hedging plants.

An arch will almost always cross a path, thus acting as a portal. It can go over a gate or be free standing. Even in a very small area, where an arch could easily be too dominant a feature, I would always try to find a suitable site, possibly against a far wall in the form of a frame for a statue, ornament or fountainhead. Certainly, there does need to be some degree of distance in order to see and appreciate an arch properly. In a reasonably sized area an arch placed, for example, in the middle distance can successfully divide a garden in two, although you must be careful that it frames something to close the vista glimpsed through it. The focal point could be an urn or sundial. A formal arch leading from a paved area of the garden to an area of informal planting can be an especially attractive feature. An arcade, which is, in fact, a multiplication of arches, also has possibilities – for instance, encircling a paved area at the intersection of four paths. Unless carefully controlled, however, multiple arches can quickly present a cluttered and over-elaborate appearance.

Living arches require slightly more patience than hedges for the very obvious reason that they must be higher, not less than 8 feet

Yew (*Taxus baccata*) is the best material of all for living arches and for hedges. It is dense and bushy and can be trimmed to a very sharp edge, but even the shaggy stage before trimming is very appealing. It has been used for these hedges and the beautifully proportioned arch – which is so generous it would take two people side by side quite comfortably. The arch is given emphasis by flanking columns of fastigiate yews. Notice that the arch has been given extra interest by the slight step up to the grassy path beyond.

1

2

(2.5 metres), to allow enough headroom for those who pass beneath them. They also require more care over training, particularly drawing together the overhead branches.

As in the case of hedges, a scale drawing should be made on card of what is proposed, cut out and put in place on the ground plan. It is an eight- to ten-year project to bring a garden arch to clipped perfection. Do not allow yourself to be put off by that fact, for it will be an immensely satisfying moment when the branches sprouting from each side are high enough to be gently drawn together and secured with string. And, once completed, you will have a stunning piece of garden architecture which will be the envy of every visitor.

Inevitably, the speediest results can be obtained by planting × *Cupressocyparis leylandii*; this will produce an arch through which you could walk in about five years. At the other end of the time scale, is slow-growing holly (*Ilex aquifolium*), which requires a good fifteen years before the full effect can be seen. Generally speaking, the most beautiful hedging plants require the most patience, but if you are going to the trouble of making an evergreen arch, it is well worth using the best material. That, of course, is yew (*Taxus baccata*). It provides by far the sturdiest evergreen arch and is the ideal plant from which to clip architectural details, such as piers, finials and so on, with which to ornament the skyline.

Beech (*Fagus sylvatica*) and hornbeam (*Carpinus betulus*), two deciduous trees sometimes used for hedging, can also make attractive living arches. They cannot be trained so precisely as yew, but they do have their own special virtues, making a dense mass of green in summer after a spring growth of exciting freshness. In winter, although they keep their leaves, they tend to lose some of their bulk, but they make up for that by glowing a warm russet when caught by the winter sunshine. Seasonal changes are certainly always more conspicuous when plants are grown as an arch rather than as a hedge.

You really must count yourself lucky if your garden already contains an arch made of brick or stone for it gives the garden a kind of distinction that, for most of us, remains unobtainable, an unrealistic dream. Building in these materials is a real extravagance. If you are accomplished at building work it may be something you can undertake yourself but, for most, it will require the services of a professional builder, very possibly working with an architect. As for the design, you might be able to copy or adapt one you admire in the neighbourhood or one illustrated in a book or magazine. Use your camera to snap references for arches, and consult the local public library. Whatever the arch's style, it should be in harmony with the house, and it can, of course, be decorated and softened by the addition of every form of climbing plant suitable for walls.

Plants trained on a solid structure, such as a masonry arch, can create an impression very similar to a living arch, particularly if the plants chosen are close-growing ones with good foliage. Of much more widespread use is the single arch of metal or wood or even, these days, of plastic,

1 Simple arching frames clothed in climbers such as roses are a useful way of introducing height into the garden, particularly if you want to avoid the dense shade created by trees. Here, an identical pair of wire arches entwined with climbing roses add much-needed form and an irrepressible charm.
2 The narrow opening in this yew arch gives a tantalizing view through to another part of the garden. Discovering a garden little by little helps sustain the viewer's interest and creates an impression that the space is bigger than it is.
3 A plain metal frame laden with clematis arching over a wooden gate is a perfect choice for a cottage garden such as this one. The materials and the style of both arch and gate go well together and suit the garden, too, but cold metal can repel plants.

3

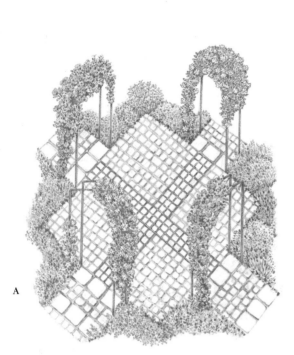

A

A Even in small gardens arches are useful devices for framing vistas and for directing the gaze above eye level. Metal arches carrying roses and clematis, plants that combine well, mark each of the paths leading from a small paved area.

B

B Yew (*Taxus baccata*), the most architectural of hedging plants, can eventually be trained to form a close-textured dark green arch. Resist the temptation to train the overhead branches until there is quite obviously adequate clearance.

1

1 An archway is a frame and it has more impact if it is darker than the picture within it, thus playing up the contrasts between light and dark. In this garden, for example, the sunny open area includes grey- and silver-leaved plants that take on a special lustre when seen through a brick arch heavily draped with dark-hued ivy. The crazy paving was an expensive mistake.
2 A brick arch such as this has no obvious practical function and is a luxury few gardeners could afford nowadays. However, it is the sort of beautiful ornamental feature that transforms a pleasant garden into something of real style and quality. The addition of a pair of finials, balls or pineapples would have enhanced its importance.

2

although I find its synthetic shiny surface out of key with whatever is planted to grow up it. The simplest of metal ones, usually with a wire mesh support, always look attractive carrying a rose such as 'Maigold' combined with a clematis. Their modesty becomes a small space, evoking as they do the Victorian villa garden.

It is unfortunate that rustic arches became a cliché of between-the-wars suburban gardening. They can be delightful, but as a type they belong squarely to the country cottage and farmhouse and definitely not to the 1920s semi-detached house. If a wooden arch is required for a town garden it should be a proper architectural arch with perhaps areas of trellis to support climbers.

The range of climbing plants is, of course, enormous and a garden arch of this kind is meant largely to be self-effacing in the interests of what it supports. But this does not mean that the material and construction are not important, since the framework of the arch will be visible for quite a long period of the year.

As the arch is a framing device the choice of flower colour is all important in relation to what is seen through it. What grows on the arch is in the foreground and must be a stronger colour than what is seen beyond it, otherwise the plants in the distance will leap out at you and the entire point of the arch will be lost. Because they are picture frames, arches can take quite strong colour – the

A magnificent leafy triumphal arch crowning a picket gate and fence between two eighteenth-century houses is a totally unexpected delight. It may have taken many years to reach its present mature state but now requires very little work to maintain. Species and cultivars of *Pyracantha*, evergreen shrubs with bright berries in autumn, or flowering plants such as forsythia could be used in much the same way.

reds, bright whites, yellows and purples – thus making what is beyond seem even further away. By planting a repeat-flowering climbing rose on one side of the arch, for instance, and a clematis with a long flowering season, such as *C. macropetala*, on the other, the arch need never be devoid of pretty bloom from late spring till early autumn.

Remember, too, the possibilities of placing, on either side of the arch, a pair of terracotta pots or urns which can act as vehicles for seasonal planting and will be beautifully set off against the background of the piers of the arch.

A selection of plants suitable for arches is given in Lists 2–4, 6–8 and 10 on pages 138–40.

ARCHITECTURE FOR PLANTS

In the past, the garden was as much, if not more, the province of the architect as of the horticulturalist. Over the centuries, many of the great innovative garden designers, such as Leon Battista Alberti (1401–72), were architects. In order to understand garden architecture, we need to place ourselves within this historical perspective. In the Victorian age, a positive battle was waged between the exponents of the landscape school, with its concern for natural effects and plants, as against the exponents of the formal garden, with its use of statuary and built features. What evolved from that debate was the classic formula which we recognize as the country house style. It used grand architectural features in vernacular materials, softened by planting of cottage garden profusion.

But this was a debate at a very high level in an age of armies of gardeners and very large gardens. How does it affect us in the era of small gardens, in the main cultivated by the owners? What happened was that gardens were considered too small to include architecture and there was an over-emphasis on plants and a lack of concern for good structural design. That is why I have deliberately called this chapter 'Architecture for Plants' and the next 'Plants as Architecture', to re-focus attention on its importance in the layout of the smallest garden.

In a great many of its aspects, garden-making is a branch of architecture, and house and garden should be considered equal partners rather than two different and opposing visual concepts. This fact should be kept very clearly in mind when planning and designing our own small gardens. Nothing makes this point more vividly than the idea of architecture for plants, for without it a whole realm of plant life, from bowers of roses to cascades of clematis, would not be shown to best advantage for they require support upon which to prosper. And, of course, a well-designed pergola or arch is there for twelve months of the year, adding vertical interest to the scene. The need for the plant support to be well-proportioned and designed hardly requires emphasis. Architecture for plants is also a vital way of marking the transition between house and garden. It can stretch out from the house walls, cleverly drawing the two together in a single, harmonious composition.

I believe in a very definite architecture for plants, which should not be in the least apologetic. Both leaf and flower are set off to far greater advantage if they contrast sharply in form with their support – a tangle of rose foliage and bloom, for example, against a geometric grid of trellis.

Climbing plants, by their very nature, can become exceedingly unruly members of the garden community, twining themselves everywhere unless they are kept in hand by sure training and capable pruning. Just as when they are set against the walls of the house they benefit from the contrast and control exerted by the architecture, the same should apply in the main body of garden itself.

Supporting plants is an important function of garden architecture, of course. But the support must be interesting and attractive in its own right, most especially where deciduous plants are concerned, so that it sets the plant off to advantage and gives character to the garden during those periods when it is bereft of bloom and foliage.

PERGOLAS & ARBOURS

A pergola, as the word implies, is Italian in origin. In the gardens of ancient Rome pergolas – stone pillars supporting a wooden roof structure – were covered with climbing plants whose leaves provided shade from the heat of the Mediterranean sun. You can see a few surviving examples among the ruins of Pompeii. Architects of the Renaissance, inspired by the writings of Pliny the Younger, who described them, extended villa gardens outwards and used pergolas as a system of interconnecting corridors. Almost without exception, these bore vines whose descendants can be seen to this day, a beautiful sight, particularly when bearing fruit or when the leaves are changing colour.

The pergola had another revival, at the beginning of this century, in the gardens designed by Sir Edwin Lutyens and Gertrude Jekyll. They deliberately used vernacular materials, old brick piers or local stone, with oak crossbeams or made of branches with the bark still on. These pergolas were devised for cooler climes, and so were less concerned with the need for shade and more with that for adding height to the garden composition and, above all, providing a wonderful vehicle for a lavish display of climbers.

An arcade is similar to a pergola but, being formed from a succession of arches, has a rounded profile – a pergola is always rectangular with a flat top.

An arbour is a shaded bower, the shade created by trained trees, shrubs or climbers. Sometimes the training will require no supports but very often a pergola-like structure will be necessary to support

A pergola gives vertical emphasis to a garden, providing support for a wide variety of climbing plants and often, as here, acting as a framing device. This pergola is extremely well built from stout squared treated timbers, and plastic mesh has been wound around the pillars to support the climbers. The planting is a classic combination of pink and white roses and clematis, which will provide a long flowering season, with white foxgloves, catmint and pink geraniums growing in the flowerbeds underneath.

1

2

1 A pergola or arcade should always lead to something, even if only to a small ornament or a plant in a pot. This arcade opens out on to a garden seat from where the pink and white roses that grow over its arches can be enjoyed to the full. The structure is made of iron with arches along the sides supporting the curving top.

2 A simple wooden pergola with a mixed planting which includes a *Rosa filipes* 'Kiftsgate' in bloom, a vine and a clematis. The advantage of such a planting is that the structure is interesting throughout the growing season. For instance, here, the rose will be at its best at midsummer, to be succeeded by the clematis and, finally, in the early autumn, by the leaves of the vine slowly turning pale yellow and then red. Notice how the lines of the pergola have been emphasized by the box hedges on both sides.

climbers that are not free standing. In a hot Mediterranean climate, the arbour is treated as a shady retreat. In more temperate areas, it can be a mistake to create shade that is too dense. It is generally better to suggest an enclosed area with light planting, preferably in a sunny part of the garden that has an attractive outlook.

A pergola or arcade should obviously not be constructed under or near a large tree, which already provides height and shade and could inhibit the growth of other plants. By its very nature, the structure should straddle a path or a paved area since grass will not grow well in shade, and you need a dry surface for walking upon.

A pergola or arcade can easily overwhelm a small garden. Even something that is modest in scale will be too dominant if placed in the centre. A good use

3

of the pergola is across a garden dividing it into two, separating, for instance, the flower from the vegetable garden. The boundary can be made more definite by infilling the area between the supports on one side of the structure with trellis. A pergola can also be run out from the back or sides of a house or the side walls or fences of a garden. This arrangement can create the secluded, restful, shady atmosphere of a cloister from which to contemplate the garden in the centre. Of course, a pergola can equally be entirely free standing. Wherever you site it, the pergola will need to lead the eye to something of interest, even if it is only a large flowerpot.

The materials used to construct a pergola or arcade can vary enormously. At one end of the scale are commercially manufactured 'tunnels' in plastic-

3 The simple style of this metal arcade is perfectly suited to the pretty potager it leads to. Vegetables and flowers – courgettes and sweet peas – have been grown over it and yellow daisies are planted underneath. A brick path runs through to a herb garden that is neatly finished with a box edging and given height with pink standard roses.

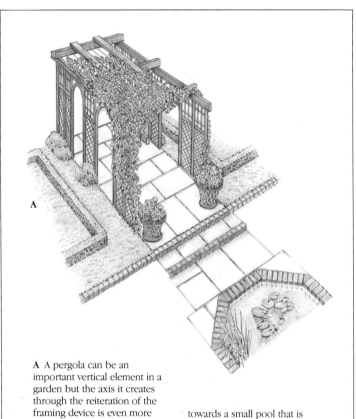

A A pergola can be an important vertical element in a garden but the axis it creates through the reiteration of the framing device is even more dominant. Here a pergola leads through a formal garden towards a small pool that is luminously bright at the end of the shaded tunnel.

B Even in a small garden a place can be found for a pergola, although to minimize the amount of shade such a structure casts it may be worth reducing the number of cross-pieces. Here a pergola has been set against one of the garden's boundaries, like a gallery giving glimpses of the garden proper.

1

1 It is easy to construct a pergola along a garden fence or wall, thus eliminating one row of supports. This method has been used to create a cloister of *Wisteria sinensis*, which can be slow growing and usually does not flower for the first one or two years – but an effect as stunning as this is well worth waiting for. Its twisted stems and branches are a pleasure in themselves in the winter months.

2 A beautifully curved free-standing arcade of iron, also dripping with wisteria. It has a very different effect to the monumental approach in the garden above, lighter and more transparent, even though both have a dazzling period of bloom and fragrance followed by an abundance of feathery leaves for the rest of summer.

covered metal but they are not beautiful and they need to be concealed by luxuriant foliage. Arcades can consist of a series of metal supports and arches or wooden supports topped by wooden arches. Metal sections may have to be custom built. Elaborately designed arcading with trellis can be very beautiful in the right place and so, too, can simple constructions of treated softwoods run up by the amateur gardener.

There is, however, a general rule which needs to be observed: the closer the pergola is to the house the more architectural it must be, built of materials related to the house. That usually means that the pillars should be of stone or reconstituted stone or brick or tiles. The crossbeams need to be of squared oak or treated softwood with timbers of small dimension for the longitudinal supports. Trellis can also be used, both for the roofing and

1 A perfumed arbour of climbing roses is a gorgeous site for a garden seat, cool and shady on a hot day. Climbers are an ideal choice for a small fenced town garden, particularly in a paved garden like this one – they take up very little ground space, and provide shelter from the elements and privacy behind luxuriant growth. Here, a tiny area has been made totally private and, at the same time, enjoys a full cycle of seasonal colour, fragrance and bloom entirely as a result of the planting of climbers on all sides.

for infilling the sides if it is necessary. Avoid using rustic pillars of bark-covered larch poles or pressure-treated softwood, which only look correct at a distance from the house. Almost invariably, too, they look wrong in town gardens. It is country gardens they suit and then only where the architectural style of the house is appropriate. Unfortunately, they are often put up in urban gardens to give a spurious rural atmosphere.

A pergola needs to be 7 to 8 feet (2.35 to 2.7 metres) in height to provide a safe clearance and be 6 to 8 feet (2 to 2.7 metres) in width. The supporting posts should be spaced 6 feet (2 metres) apart and will require wire or wire mesh to support climbers that are not, like *wisteria sinensis*, naturally strong twiners. Do not stint on the timbers, otherwise the plants will lack the support which they will need to thrive. And remember that the drawback to inexpensive materials is that they do not last.

As to planting, there the excitement really begins, for the effects can range from one dazzling short-lived display to a carefully selected range of climbers giving visual and perfumed pleasure over the whole year. A decision to opt for a single annual tableau is perhaps too limiting in a small garden, although it is a perfectly valid one.

My own preference in a small space would be to stagger the effects over a longer period of the growing season. If the pergola is to bear roses only, choose climbers with a long flowering period. The scented 'Gloire de Dijon', with its pale apricot and yellow tints has a long flowering season. Another rose which it is difficult to beat is 'Iceberg', sweet-scented and providing a cascade of snow-white flowers also over a long period.

The interest a pergola can have through the year is increased by the introduction of other climbing plants, such as the evergreen clematis *C. armandii* and the various vines, of which *Vitis* 'Brandt' has exceptionally rich autumn colouring. If the climate is not too cold, do not forget the passion flower (*Passiflora caerulea*), with its extraordinary pale green flowers streaked with purple succeeded by orange fruits. In fact, let your fancy range but remember always to adhere strictly to the pruning instructions or your pergola will be less clothed with bloom than you had envisaged.

Plants suitable for pergolas and arbours are given in Lists 2–4 and 9–11 on pages 138–40.

2 A magnificent 'natural' arbour formed by pleached limes (*Tilia*). This delightful shady retreat is the ideal place for a garden seat, for quiet reflection out of the hot sun. The limes have been trained over a framework of wood in order to achieve this effect. They are fast growing and wonderfully fragrant.

3 There is no doubt that eating food out of doors is often a memorable experience in fine weather. A pergola can be simply erected to provide an alfresco dining-room. Here, a single battered column has been used to support wooden beams that radiate out from the corner of a walled garden; the result is a leafy outdoor room. The fluted column is encircled by a grape vine and a nearby wall is covered with a fig – symbols of the essential culinary and horticultural arts.

TRELLIS & PLANT SUPPORTS

*M*any plants, such as honeysuckle, clematis and ivy, require some support upon which to grow. This can, of course, be met in the most rudimentary manner by an arbitary insertion of poles and bamboo canes but to do so bypasses all the opportunities for creating really spectacular effects with interesting plant supports.

Trellis is perhaps the very best material to use. The way it was used in the past makes our approach today seem very timid and utilitarian. It had become one of the key ingredients of garden making by the middle of the seventeenth century. Pictures and engravings of that period are full of ideas for how to use it. Enclosed areas, or cabinets, as they were called, were made of trellis, as were arbours, pergolas, summerhouses and, more unexpectedly, free-standing plant supports in the form of columns, pillars and obelisks.

The simplest support of all is a stake driven into the earth to which the plant is tied. In the case of a standard rose the stake will be a permanent part of the composition, so it should be of good proportion, be treated with a wood preservative that will not harm the plant, and the tie must be a seemly one. Good sturdy bamboo canes always look right so keep a plentiful supply of them to hand. Supports for tall herbaceous plants are integral parts of the border picture, too. Circles of metal lattice with legs that can be pushed into the ground give support throughout the growing season. They are put into position in early spring so that the plant grows up through the centre, its new foliage quickly camouflaging the support. In a flower border a pretty effect can be had by propping up floppy

Plant supports can be telling features in a garden's composition. The four arbours in Sir Geoffrey Jellicoe's Paradise Garden at Sutton Place, Surrey, like every other aspect of the garden, have been chosen with great taste and sensitivity. They are made of painted ironwork and were specially designed and constructed for this location. Less expensive versions can be built of wood and trellis. They have been lightly clad with sweet-smelling climbers to highlight the delicate framework and the elegant fountain.

1 Inexpensive commercially manufactured trellis, treated with wood preservative, has been used in the simplest possible manner to transform an otherwise uninteresting corridor at the side of a house. Two arches, the nearest bearing a vine, straddle the path, making the area seem wider than it really is. The use of two arches, rather than one, accentuates the perspective and frames the garden at the end of the path.
2 Both solid and transparent fencing have been used to extremely good effect to create this garden within a garden. The woven fencing to the right not only protects the crops from the elements but carries espaliered fruit trees, while an ornamental rose grows over the broad-gauge trellis, which could also serve as a support for vegetables such as beans or courgettes.

3 A custom-made trellis, which is built with a broad mesh, has been painted white to match the heavily scented white jasmine (*Jasminum officinale*) that it is supporting, and to contrast sharply with the foliage behind. Using a plant support such as this trellis as a divider in a garden is often more appropriate than having a solid wall because it looks lighter and more elegant. More importantly, it also means that it is possible to see glimpses of the flowers and foliage, the hedges and trees, that lie in the garden beyond it.

plants with a tangle of twigs. At Sissinghurst Castle, the garden created by Vita Sackville-West and Harold Nicolson, plants such as rosemary that have spilled out beyond their confines are lifted up by miniature hurdles made of chestnut. Make sure that the ties are green string or wire to blend in.

In addition to these very plain and practical supports, there are more fanciful wooden ones that certainly contribute to the overall mood of the garden. Indeed, rose supports provide the opportunity for much invention. Pillars and columns, obelisks and pyramids all make very attractive supports. They can be as simple as a framework made of treated softwoods or as elaborate as one painted white with the sides infilled with trellis. Metal can be used in exactly the same way but it is expensive and would have to be custom made. It is

a durable choice, although it has the disadvantage that, being cold, plants may be repelled by it.

The use of these kinds of architectural support for clematis, honeysuckle, a rose or other climber is not only practical but, if well made and designed, they will give you something beautiful to look at for all twelve months of the year. Such features, in groups of two or four, could easily form the dominant motifs holding together a small garden. Although their height demands that they should be pegged down to avoid being blown over in the wind, it is a good idea not to cement them into position so you have the chance to re-position them if you are unhappy with the original site or to simply move them for a season.

A word about colour. Off-whites, greys and greens are the best choices – they do not distract attention from the plants. Treated timber always looks presentable in the garden but it is usual to paint the more complex structures. This does present a problem when they need to be re-painted for plants will have to be removed.

One of the reasons for growing plants over supports is to give the garden height and, hence, visual interest. Trellis does this to very great effect. Unfortunately, it is both under- and over-used. When used to excess, the whole garden seems to become a forest of wooden mesh and the result is far from pleasing; it certainly detracts from the plants. Nevertheless, trellis offers the most wonder-ful opportunities for really cheap garden architec-ture, for dividing walls and screens within the garden as well as decorative application to the walls of the house. Each use produces a different optical effect: against a wall it makes a two-dimensional

pattern across a flat surface; as a barrier it creates a perforated wall which can only be seen through in any detail really close to. It is indeed its transparent lacy quality that makes trellis such an asset in the garden for all kinds of effects.

The trellis generally available is often badly made with too wide a mesh and offers a very poor investment. The very cheap expandable kind should be avoided except for the most transitory uses. The trellis found in garden centres and builders' yards should be very carefully examined before you buy it, to check the quality of both its wood and its making. It comes in square or diamond-shaped mesh and usually in sections of a set size, and the wood is either treated or left untreated. There are, however, specialist manu-facturers who offer a wider range of ready-made pieces with a closer mesh, in more interesting

1

2

1 Trellis is often more interesting when painted colours other than the traditional white. Here, a subtle, dark blue-grey sets off the rich, deep red colour of the rose to great advantage. If the trellis had been white, the rose might have seemed rather strident.

2 Although this trellis is painted the same colour as the one on the left, it looks quite different set against a white-washed wall and supporting a number of roses, in whites, pinks and reds.

3 These handsome, free-standing rose supports are made of iron and painted black. They have been arranged in pairs in this very stylish, small new garden that is full of eye-catching details, from the brick path with its slight changes in level to the mophead acacias (*Robinia pseudoacacia* 'Inermis') and the just visible simple bench placed to the right beneath the young yew hedge. (The frontispiece also illustrates this particular garden.)

Many roses, particularly some of the splendid old varieties, are of very loose and sprawling habit. A simple metal frame provides a neat and inconspicuous support in the growing season.

3

1

2

1 Clematis macropetala is a vigorous, bushy climber with an abundance of blue or violet-blue flowers. Here, flower-laden, it is grown as a pillar, up wire mesh encircling a post driven into the ground.

2 Variegated ivy looks very dramatic trained over this metal garden arch that spans the path. Ivy is reasonably fast growing – it would have only taken about three to four years to reach this height – and clothes this important vertical garden feature for the whole twelve months of the year.

3 A classic sight in old-fashioned gardens, this old fruit tree is used to support a rampant rambler, the charming white-flowered *Rosa filipes* 'Kiftsgate'. This cascading effect lasts for only a few weeks in the height of summer when the rose blooms, but the display is prodigious and deliciously fragrant.

shapes – having a Gothic arch at the top, for instance, or finials at the corners. This is obviously more expensive and should be used for permanent features rather than temporary ones.

Whenever you consider using trellis you must measure the area to be covered and marry this to the available standard sections. This may mean adapting what is available to achieve the effect you are aiming at. A rough scale drawing is always a sensible thing to do, marking on it the sections and building on to the overall pattern with walls, windows and arches to link the sections.

There are many ways of creating patterns and architectural shapes using trellis in conjunction with supporting posts and crossbeams. But do remember that trellis requires looking after and eventually total renewal. As part of a long-term

3

garden strategy where budget is a prime consideration trellis can, however, offer a stylish short-term solution until the grand scheme is affordable.

Taken to the limits, trellis can be used as the major design ingredient of a garden, and is especially suitable for town gardens or for small courtyards. It can be mounted on to every wall or just confined to the one opposite the house. Ambitious schemes using trellis need to be planned in detail and professional help would probably be needed to divide the area into archways and to erect pillars and other features, including trompe l'œil effects. When trellis is used as architecture, its pattern and the shapes it forms should not be obscured by excessive planting.

A long narrow garden can be delightfully divided with screens of fine-mesh trellis, from a distance giving the appearance of transparent gauzes. Screens with linking arches can enclose a section of a garden to make a secret area or equally they can be used to build up interest at the intersection of paths. In a new garden, trellis provides immediate height while hedges, trees and shrubs have yet to grow; use it while the hedge is growing and remove it as the hedge nears completion. Very pretty effects can be got, too, by using trellis as low fencing, for example, either enclosing sections of a garden or a flowerbed. After all, it is a good idea to remember that, to be effective, the trellis does not have to be 6 feet (2 metres) high.

Trellis has great potential in the vegetable garden, too, being able to transform that humble patch into an ornamental potager. Enclosing walls of trellis will provide support for runner beans and

for trained fruit trees while the simplest of pavilions can be constructed as a focal point to take climbers and give the potager much needed height.

Another invaluable use of trellis is in the construction of all kinds of arbours. It can be a very simple structure, literally three sections of trellis for the walls, linked by square timbers at the top and, perhaps, with a triangular pediment at the front. A few slats could be added to form a roof and give support to climbers. The result would not have been out of place in an Elizabethan garden. Plant a sweet-smelling rose, such as 'Aloha', and jasmine on either side to complete the scene.

Plants can support other plants, of course. *Tropaeolum speciosum*, for instance, can bring scarlet blooms trailing through a dark yew hedge in high summer. There are many other scramblers, including some of the clematis, that are most at home twining their way through living supports. Old fruit trees, unpruned and long past fruit growing, are ideal for holding up rambler roses.

This simple country garden of flowers, herbs and vegetables requires height, but a garden ornament would be pretentious and out of place. Instead, during the summer months, tall bamboo wigwams are erected to carry runner beans which will have scarlet flowers before they crop.

The roses should be planted about 6 feet (2 metres) from the trunk and trained by a cane or ropes up to the branches. A vigorous rambler can, in time, totally engulf the tree and bring it down so it is important to keep watch for signs of danger and introduce wooden posts to prop it up if need be. There is no shortage of rampant growers with which to achieve this effect, from the slightly tender *Rosa longicuspis*, with its huge sprays of creamy white flowers, to the beloved 'Albertine', which can deck a tree with salmon pink bloom.

Plants benefitting from the support of trellis are given in Lists 2–4 and 10 on pages 138–40.

PLANTS AS ARCHITECTURE

Nothing more truly draws on the gardens of the past than the concept of plants as architecture. Throughout the sixteenth and seventeenth centuries, the garden was conceived as an arrangement of spaces, forms and surfaces achieved by the planting, trimming and pruning of nature into geometric shapes and patterns. Plants were architecture and green sculpture was placed in much the same way as a stone column, pedestal, plinth or statue. Trees were marshalled into avenues, circles, squares and triangles on a ground plan and clipped into pyramids, obelisks, domes or columns in elevation. And this treatment was not reserved for plants we still associate with clipping, such as yew or box, but trees such as elms and acacias. 'Our trees rise in cones, globes and pyramids. We see the marks of the scissors upon every plant and bush,' Joseph Addison wrote in 1712, when an attack on the ridiculous and extravagant excesses of this type of formal gardening was under way.

The most famous garden of this type to survive, although its topiary was re-cut in the early nineteenth century, is at Levens Hall in Cumbria. It is a fantastic arrangement of hedges and clipped evergreens, including a king with a crown on his head, a crowned lion with a flamboyant tail, Queen Elizabeth with her maids of honour, even an arbour called 'The Judge's Wig'. This is on the grand scale but in its own age it was a style perfectly attuned to small gardens.

There is much to learn from a study of the elements of the old formal gardens which depend on the arts of topiary, training, pleaching and pollarding in order to achieve their astonishing effects. The use of evergreens and the fascinating skeletal shapes of trained plants mean that these grand formal schemes hold their interest throughout the year when the leaf and flower interplanted into the green pattern has long since vanished – ideas that lend themselves perfectly to the small garden where interest through from late autumn to early spring must be very carefully planned. Although topiary, pollarding and training are the techniques for making architecture from plants, do not forget those plants which without any or very little attention achieve an identical effect. The Irish yew (*Taxus baccata* 'Fastigiata') forms a splendid slow-growing column of evergreens (the golden variety, *T. b.* 'Fastigiata Aureamarginata', is even slower). It can be used in pairs to frame a vista or planted in greater numbers to form a short avenue. Although *Juniper commununis* 'Hibernica', the Irish juniper, needs tying in, it too is an erect and stately formal tree.

Architectural plants, like the parts of a building, need to be placed as though they are performing a function, albeit also ornamental. Interestingly, they are rarely successful when standing alone. A single architectural plant in an informal group may add height and accent and provide a focal point, but it will not be pure architecture; only when it is contributing to the bones of a formal scheme – as one of a pair, for instance, or in a symmetrical group or as one of an avenue – will it become that.

TOPIARY

*A*nyone who has seen one of the great Italian or French formal gardens, such as the Villa d'Este at Tivoli or Versailles, or one of the romantic compositions of Victorian England – the tableau depicting the Sermon on the Mount at Packwood House, for instance – could not fail to be utterly enchanted by any of these triumphs of man, shears and secateurs in hand, over nature. The spectacular impact of these gardens depends almost entirely on what is known as the art of topiary, which the dictionary usefully defines as 'clipping and trimming shrubs, etc. into ornamental or fantastic shapes'. It is an art that has not been confined to grand gardens. We still see examples today of folk topiary: a yew clipped into a cup and saucer or a giant bird presiding over a pretty cottage garden. These make the point well that topiary is full of potential for even the smallest space. And it is rich in history; it was the Romans who first clipped and pruned trees and shrubs 'into ornamental and fantastic shapes'. The word *topiarus*, according to Cicero, referred to the ornamental gardener, who belonged to the highest class of slave.

The scale of the large topiary gardens can be offputting: their effects seem to be beyond the capacity of the ordinary gardener impatient for a result that requires a long programme of maintenance. But a word of encouragement. Topiary in the small garden needs to be small and hence mature effects can be achieved reasonably quickly. Depending on size, these can take anything between eight and ten years, although the intent will be clear after three. And there is nothing against cheating a little, for both box

A perfect example of the use of topiary to achieve year-round structure and interest in an essentially seasonal garden, in this case a herb garden. From spiky rosemary to feathery fennel, herbs are untidy members of the garden community and the success of this garden depends on the strong framework provided by the yew hedge, and the symmetrical planting of four balls of a golden form of box (*Buxus sempervirens*) at the centrepoint and the four contrasting green box corkscrews.

(Buxus sempervirens) and bay (*Laurus nobilis*) are available ready trained in the form of cones, balls, pyramids and standards. They are an extravagance but give instant effect.

Fantasy can run riot with topiary but, in a small garden, I think it is most sensitively and stylishly used in the form of geometric shapes which are satisfying in themselves by virtue of their perfect proportions: balls, cones, cubes, pyramids, tetrahedrons or a combination of two or more of these basic shapes.

These forms of topiary are essential ingredients of the formal garden, particularly the parterre, when they can be combined with more elaborate and eccentric shapes. They are equally at home

1 Variegated holly (*Ilex x altaclaerensis* 'Golden King') clipped into a dome on top of a sphere is a handsome feature, particularly in winter.
2 Four box balls grouped at the foot of a tree with self-seeded lady's mantle (*Alchemilla mollis*) delicately breaking any excessive formality.
3 Yew (*Taxus baccata*) treated in a highly original way, its branches exposed and its leaves confined to tufted mounds, the new growth a velvet pile.

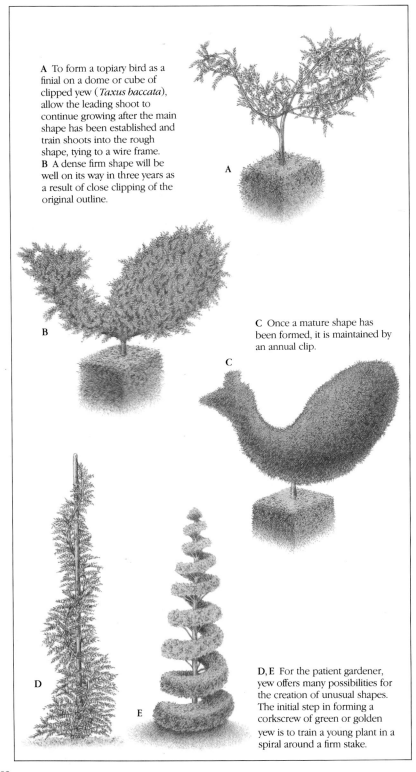

A To form a topiary bird as a finial on a dome or cube of clipped yew (*Taxus baccata*), allow the leading shoot to continue growing after the main shape has been established and train shoots into the rough shape, tying to a wire frame.
B A dense firm shape will be well on its way in three years as a result of close clipping of the original outline.

C Once a mature shape has been formed, it is maintained by an annual clip.

D, E For the patient gardener, yew offers many possibilities for the creation of unusual shapes. The initial step in forming a corkscrew of green or golden yew is to train a young plant in a spiral around a firm stake.

used as punctuation marks amidst the happy profusion of a cottage planting. But topiary belongs not only to the gardens of nostalgia. Its geometric shapes are eternal and can perfectly suit a garden conceived purely in terms of this century, whether Art Deco or even Post-modernist. Why not copy a Henry Moore in box or yew?

Every plant should be plotted on your ground plan, cut out to scale in card and arranged on it so that you can consider the exciting effects of distance and height which each can add. Remember that for the most successful effects topiary must be planned from the outset as part of the unchanging structure of the garden.

A series of pyramids or cones flanking a pathway draws the eye into the distance, making the space seem greater than it really is. If the topiary is gradually reduced in scale from a particular viewpoint, you will achieve what is known as false perspective, giving an impression of even more space. A pair can act as entrance piers leading into a garden or an area of it, perhaps framing a 'picture' or a summerhouse or seat. Groups can give splendid emphasis and form to a focal point – four identical shapes, for instance, arranged symmetrically around a sundial or garden statue. A single bold topiary shape can be the focal point of an entire garden but, in general, it is best to place them in pairs or groups.

All of these design effects can also be achieved using plants in wooden or fibreglass tubs or terracotta pots. Box or bay are the most successful plants suitable for clipping that can be grown in containers. The scale is generally smaller than it would be if their roots were in the ground but with pot-grown plants you have the advantage that they can be arranged at will to enliven even the dullest areas. Topiary is almost exclusively executed in evergreens. The two chief plants are yew (*Taxus baccata*) and box. Both require annual clipping, yew in late summer, box in late spring. The rich dark green of yew, when cut into a geometric

Movable topiary trophies: a standard bay tree (*Laurus nobilis*) with a corkscrew trunk – a magnificent specimen that has been formed by twisting the trunk around a stake, a feat of training which, alas, has taken many years to achieve – and a line of box balls in terracotta pots, like sentinels. What makes this collection the more charming is the fact that it, and even the little putto, can be moved and rearranged elsewhere in the garden.

shape, responds marvellously to the play of light. So does box. Its leaf is lighter in colour and smaller and it has a delectable scent. But it grows much more slowly than yew; it should not be used for any large projects unless you are prepared to wait a couple of decades. Bay can also be used but its large leaf precludes any complex training and, unlike the other two, a sharp winter can kill it.

Holly (species and cultivars of *Ilex*) can be used and the variegated varieties are particularly striking. I recommend especially the broad-leaved 'Golden King' with its rich yellow margin to the leaves. The Portugal laurel (*Prunus lusitanica*) can be cut to form a stately umbrella and evergreen varieties of euonymus (for example *E. fortunei* 'Emerald Gaiety') can be trained into standards.

Deciduous plants cannot be clipped to such precise shapes as evergreens and you will have to accept them either leafless or with a change of hue in winter. Their other disadvantage is that they grow too quickly out of shape and will thus require clipping more than once during the growing season. The best of these plants are beech (*Fagus sylvatica*), hornbeam (*Carpinus betulus*) and common quickthorn (*Crataegus monogyna*).

The satisfaction that topiary gives is well worth waiting for; when it comes it will be year-long. The clipped shapes of trees provide the ideal contrast to transient spring and summer foliage and bloom and in winter they reign supreme, looking extraordinary even under snow.

A selection of plants suitable for topiary is given in List 11 on page 140.

This ravishing little garden in the form of a box parterre is divided into compartments with gravel paths. The box cones and domes emphasize the symmetrical pattern, providing interesting shape and height, as do the four standard roses in the centre bed around a little stone trophy.

A A
B B
C C

A A simple knot suitable for a small garden could easily take the addition of pot-grown topiary, for example, arranged in pairs at each of the four openings.

B Topiary really is the perfect accompaniment to this very ingenious knot garden, the balls and cones providing accents to a design that might otherwise be difficult to read unless viewed from a higher vantage point. The interlacing pattern is made more distinct by having strands planted in varieties of box (*Buxus sempervirens*) chosen for their contrasting colour.

C The intricate pattern of this knot garden could easily be obscured by the addition of topiary but it would go well in a formal setting that also featured topiary.

TRAINING PLANTS

*T*he techniques for training plants can be used to great advantage
in the smallest garden. Training means control and is, therefore,
ideally suited to a limited space. It makes possible the use of some
large plants which, if allowed to grow unchecked, would take over
the entire garden space – for instance, holm or evergreen oak
(*Quercus ilex*) can be grown on a single stem with a rounded or
umbrella-shaped head; flowering thorn (*Crataegus*) is much easier
to handle when clipped, and plants such as *Eucalyptus gunnii* can be
coppiced, that is, cut back to make a bush. There are many rather
formless plants, such as species and cultivars of firethorn (*Pyracantha*), that are vastly improved by being trained, and others that
will flower or fruit more profusely. And, in formal gardens, the tighter,
firmer shapes are more appropriate than the tumbling, airy look of
untrained plants.

Training is an intriguing exercise, persuading plants to grow in
precisely the way you want them to. It holds enormous appeal
because of its basis in controlled form and its interesting variety of
effects – for instance, roses on rope swags, ivy on frames, ornamental
fruit trees, pollarding and pleaching, and controlled climbers such as
wisteria and clematis. The most extreme form is topiary in which
trees are given sculptural or architectural shape. The actual training is
not particularly difficult, although it does call for commitment.

Fruit trees remain an extremely under-utilized ingredient of the
small garden, in spite of their ornamental and culinary value. The
development of very dwarfing rootstocks has meant that it is even

Fruit trees are capable of being trained into extremely
decorative patterns, a way of growing them particularly favoured
by French gardeners in the seventeenth century.
The trees can be trained against a fence or wall or, as here,
on a frame – in this instance of iron stakes with wires
stretched between in parallel lines. This apple
has been pruned to form a double-u, technically known
as a palmette. The mature shape could have taken eight to
ten years to develop; fruit trees grown as cordons would have
created a screen more quickly.

1

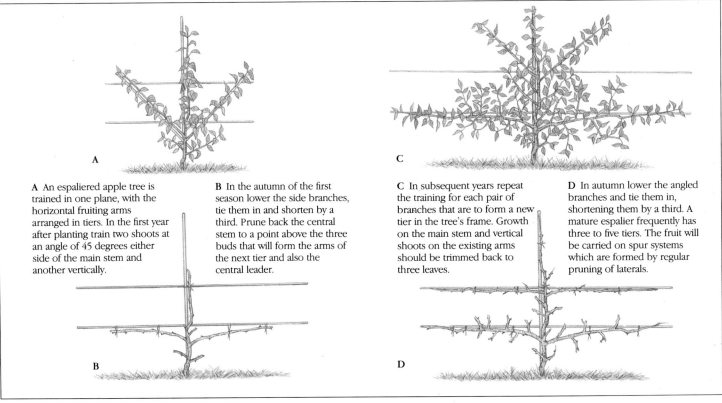

A An espaliered apple tree is trained in one plane, with the horizontal fruiting arms arranged in tiers. In the first year after planting train two shoots at an angle of 45 degrees either side of the main stem and another vertically.

B In the autumn of the first season lower the side branches, tie them in and shorten by a third. Prune back the central stem to a point above the three buds that will form the arms of the next tier and also the central leader.

C In subsequent years repeat the training for each pair of branches that are to form a new tier in the tree's frame. Growth on the main stem and vertical shoots on the existing arms should be trimmed back to three leaves.

D In autumn lower the angled branches and tie them in, shortening them by a third. A mature espalier frequently has three to five tiers. The fruit will be carried on spur systems which are formed by regular pruning of laterals.

2

3

possible to grow suitably grafted small fruit trees in pots or tubs. Therefore, there is no excuse for a small garden to be devoid of its own fruit and the lingering prejudice against intermingling fruit and flowers or fruit and vegetables should be rejected. Trained fruit trees could be used as screens – for example, a row of cordon apple trees separating a potager from an ornamental section – or to compartmentalize the whole garden.

Fruit trees can be trained decoratively either flat – against a wall or fence, for example – or in a free-standing shape but this last treatment is now rather uncommon. When fruit trees are trained flat, they can be fixed to a frame of wood and wire, or if they are to be against a wall or fence, their branches can be tied to a network of wires attached to the wall surface. Many fruit trees will benefit from being grown against a warm, sun-drenched wall, although some, including the morello cherry, can be grown in less favourable positions.

For a fan shape, the branches are trained in one plane, spreading outwards from a single point low down on the trunk. Building up the initial structure of the fan takes time so trees are often bought ready-trained from nurseries. Apples, pears, cherries, nectarines, apricots and plums all lend themselves to this treatment. The use of other

1 These espaliered apple trees have been pruned to form a two-tiered fence. Fruit can be produced in the smallest of spaces by ingenious training. Apples can even be planted as an edging to a path or around a vegetable garden. All that is required is a supporting structure such as these low wooden fences on which to tie the branches. Notice how trees are grown, back to back, on both sides of the frame.
2 A part-view of a free-standing, fan-trained apple tree. Fans are usually grown against a wall or a rectangular wire framework, the main support being supplemented by bamboo canes that radiate out from the trunk creating a fan shape to which the branches are tied. There are a number of other fruit trees that can be grown in fans, in particular pears, peaches and morello cherries.
3 It is often difficult to introduce height into a vegetable garden. In this potager, the problem has been solved by pruning a gooseberry bush into a standard. Although, nowadays, gooseberries are generally grown as bushes, in the nineteenth century they were frequently trained into shapes. Here, the magnificent standard gooseberry, in fruit, is treated formally, combined with round balls of box.

A In pleaching, a technique of training trees such as lime (*Tilia*) and hornbeam (*Carpinus betulus*) in a single plane, young trees are planted at regular intervals in a line and branches that will make horizontal tiers are tied in to supporting wires.

B An avenue formed by two rows of pleached limes or hornbeams forms an impressive axis to a garden and can be adapted to schemes on quite a small scale. Pleached hornbeams make a denser aerial hedge than limes.

2

kinds of training in one plane – the espalier, the cordon and the u – is perhaps best confined to either apple or pear trees.

In espalier training the branches extend horizontally from a single stem; they are arranged in pairs at intervals of about 18 inches (45 centimetres), generally forming three to five tiers. A cordon is single stemmed and trained either to grow vertically or leaning at an angle of 45 degrees. Its side shoots and fruiting spurs are kept short and, generally, it will be producing fruit by its second or third year. Cordons are usually planted in a series and, because they require little space, are particularly suited to small gardens. U-shape patterns are made by training the branches symmetrically outwards and then upwards to make a variety of shapes with self-explanatory names: palmette, double u-shape or candelabrum.

One long-term project, if there is space, is a fruit tunnel. This calls for very rigorous pruning or else

1 Broad-leaved trees such as lime, beech and hornbeam can be trained to achieve interesting architectural effects. Here, lime (*Tilia* species or cultivar) has been planted beside a wall and pleached into a single strand – the effect is of windows with the trunks acting as glazing bars. All that is required after the structure has been formed is annual clipping. The landscape in summer will be framed by green.
2 Pleached limes trained to form a cloistered walk, which is wonderfully fragrant in summer. It has been grown over a frame constructed of supports and cross-pieces to make a tunnel. The limes were then planted between the supports and, when their branches reached the right height, were trained over and tied to the horizontals. This technique could be used to make a delightful pleached lime arbour in the corner of quite a small garden.

you will be left with bare sections of trunk. Such a tunnel is grown on a wooden or plastic-covered metal frame, which should be about 7 feet high and 6 feet wide (2.3 and 2 metres) with the trees planted every 27 to 30 inches (65 to 70 centimetres). The tunnel requires two-year-old apple or pear trees on semi-dwarfing rootstocks.

It is essential to start with good stock from a reliable nursery. For apples, the most commonly used rootstock for cordons, espaliers and fans is the semi-dwarfing MM. 106 which, when fully grown as a free-standing tree, results in a branch spread of some 10 to 13 feet (3 to 4 metres); less frequently, the dwarfing M. 26 is used. The more dwarfing rootstock M. 9 and the extremely dwarfing M. 27 are generally used for potted trees. Quince C and Quince A are the most commonly used rootstocks for trained pears.

One way to produce a tall, leafy screen is by pleaching, a form of training broad-leaved trees very popular in France. Pleached trees can make an ideal green enclosure or screen in summer and in winter there is the beauty of the regular geometric framework of the branches to contemplate. Pleached trees are also used to form avenues. The trees are pruned very severely so that growth is restricted to the top on one plane and then their branches are trained to interlace.

Young trees should be planted at intervals of 10 feet (3.3 metres) tied to stakes between 10 and 12 feet (3.3 and 4 metres) high. The trunks are pruned

2

1 Seasonal pruning is part of the training that has made this clematis, 'Perle d'Azur', a spectacular curtain of bloom in summer and autumn and a wonderful backdrop to a weathered garden seat. It should be pruned very severely in midwinter by cutting back the whole of the previous year's growth.
2 A simple iron framework of arches and linking swags forms a circular pergola. Along this framework pink and white roses have been trained with careful attention to their pruning to ensure flowers from top to bottom and along the linking swags. The white rose is the rambler 'Rambling Rector', which has small flowers in clusters and blooms only once a year.
3 Wisteria sinensis makes a superb display, and it looks its best against a pale wall. It is an extremely vigorous climber and can grow up to 100 feet (30 metres). However, it does need careful training as here, the branches being tied on to wires attached in parallel lines to vine hooks embedded in the mortar. To get this kind of flowering, pruning back to two or three buds is essential in autumn or winter.

3

This rather charming portable mock topiary is formed by variegated ivy being trained up a metal frame in the form of a corkscrew. The method could be applied to any shape constructed out of strong wire. I have seen it done on a large scale to great effect: forming elephants and dragons in a children's playground.

up to 6 feet (2 metres). Above that a series of wires are stretched from stake to stake at intervals of not less than a foot (30 centimetres), depending on how dense you wish the screen to be. Branches are then trained out along the wires and, eventually, are tied together so that they become entwined. Be careful only to go to a height which is manageable for annual pruning. The usual tree for pleaching is the common lime (*Tilia platyphyllos*), including the red-twigged form 'Rubra', or a hybrid, *T. × euchlora*, which is less troubled by aphids.

A similar effect can be attained by a variation of pleaching, resulting in a 'stilt', hedge, a neat rectangular clipped hedge supported on the bare stems of trees planted at regular intervals. On a small scale such a hedge could make an interesting addition to a garden of modest size. The tree most commonly used is the hornbeam (*Carpinus betulus*). By careful pruning a good leafy head is encouraged to develop at about 6 to 8 feet (2 to 2.7 metres) from the ground and is then clipped to form a tight cube, a perfect aerial hedge that is green in summer and copper in winter.

Pollarding is a somewhat brutal method of training certain broadleaved trees – for example, species and cultivars of lime (*Tilia*), plane (*Platanus*), poplar (*Populus*) and willow (*Salix*) – in which the growth of the main trunk or large branches is permanently checked. The very thin branches that develop at the point or points where the main growth is held are cut back regularly, causing the terminals to develop a characteristically swollen and knotty appearance. Formerly the principal reason for pollarding was economic but this method of training is also frequently used for ornamental effect.

Many roses are available as standards – and the best of the ramblers as weeping standards – a way of growing roses that allows plenty of scope for formal arrangements. Rambling roses with pliant stems can be trained to the soft curving shapes of looped ropes; although most flower only once a year, they make a wonderful display over a reasonably long period. Some climbing roses, such as 'Madame Alfred Carrière', are as vigorous growers as wisteria and clematis and, like these plants, benefit from careful training in the initial stages when their framework is being established.

A selection of plants suitable for training is given in Lists 2–4 and 10–13 on pages 138–41.

FOCAL POINTS
& EYE-CATCHERS

Focal points relate closely to something essential in good design; an appreciation of how the human eye actually looks at the space around it. Since the Renaissance, garden design has been concerned with the articulation of space based upon the rules of perspective: that converging lines mean distance and that colour softens in tone the further away it is from the onlooker. Both points have been exploited by garden-makers, either by deliberately distorting the lines of hedges or paths in false perspective to make them seem longer than they really are or by placing strong colour in the foreground and soft at the furthest point to make the latter appear even more distant than it actually is.

The manipulation of space also works from a premise that the eye is always being led towards something. That is why focal points are fundamental to any successful garden composition. A path leading nowhere is devoid of interest. It calls for a seat, a summerhouse or an ornament to lure us onwards. A garden always needs focal points, be it a topiary yew, a sundial or a fountain, or something as simple as a carefully placed terracotta container – to hold its visual structure together from several viewpoints and to make what we all strive to achieve – a garden which is a series of breathtaking pictures.

The great terraced garden at Powys Castle in Gwent offers one of the most perfect instances of the use of focal points in garden design that I know. On the piers of the balustrading of the main terrace half way down the hillside, four lead statues of shepherds and shepherdesses are placed. They seem to dance as they joyously hold together the whole composition of that vast garden which not only stretches above but below them. We can look down on the figures from an upper terrace where they preside over the garden that spreads beneath, and it is also possible to look up at them from a lower terrace, set against a counterfoil of stately Italianate architecture. We can also see them on their own level where they appear silhouetted against the distant hills of the landscape in which the castle is situated. These four beautiful ornaments are meant to be viewed from every angle, front, back and sides, and are as effective displayed against a backdrop of evergreens as one of weathered brick and stone, and are also ideally placed to respond fully to the subtle movement of light on their sculptured form both by day and by night.

Owners of small gardens tend to shy off focal points as though they had no place in a more modest scheme of things and were the prerogative only of very large and grand gardens. It would be a pity, though, to deny yourself an interesting element of garden-making which can give such enormous pleasure.

Focal points reflect the old tradition that the garden is as much the province of the architect as the horticulturalist. But sadly, on account of soaring costs for capital building works and an obsession with planting, the roles of architect and sculptor have been diminished if not totally obliterated. The future of this rich tradition now lies in the hands of the designer of small gardens; its essence may have to be distilled but it is still capable of imaginative and sensitive application, even to the tiniest of spaces.

ORNAMENTS & SUNDIALS

*G*arden ornaments at their best are decorative and sometimes very beautiful, essential elements in the composition of the totally successful garden design – but they must also have a meaning. It is a lesson we can learn from the past, when an ornament was chosen to embody the 'spirit of the place' and was not mere decoration. A statue of Venus was meant to evoke love and the golden age of classical mythology, a bust of Hercules the heroic virtues, and a sundial mortality and the passing of time.

This is a point worth remembering now that a revival of the use of ornament is taking place. For over half a century we have suffered the devastating effects of a reaction to centuries of tradition. Inside the house plaster mouldings, patterned tiling, stained glass and decorative detailing in wood, all of which drew on forms from the repertory of ornament going back thousands of years, was thrown out. The effect on garden design was equally catastrophic. The basic elements which designers had used since the Renaissance were abandoned, resulting, at its most extreme, in the garden being reduced to an expanse of concrete paving with ornament in the form of a few undecorated containers and a single piece of contemporary sculpture, often in stainless steel. Fortunately, that phase has passed but the re-establishment of a new tradition of garden sculpture and ornament remains a challenge for the future.

Garden ornament should not be an afterthought. The fact that in some books on garden design it turns up in a final chapter covering 'accessories' is the result of a plant-orientated design philosophy that

The composition of this formal garden, in which many shades of green are combined with all-white blooms, depends on the sundial as its central focal point. I would have favoured a more robust column as a support but that is a minor defect in a design which flows naturally outwards from the ornament – its round shape repeated in the circle of stone setts on which it stands and then in the box hedges which encircle it and tame the lovely tangled mass of plants in the flowerbeds. The cypresses emphasize the formality of the layout.

A

A Simple geometric shapes in reconstituted stone are among the best of the new ornaments available. A pair of obelisks flanking a path help to concentrate the view.

B

B A large terracotta jar can make a simple and dignified ornament. It could be used in many positions, set on a pedestal in a paved court, as here, or in a hedge recess.

C

C In a small garden, or in a corner of a larger one, a free-standing ornament might take up too much space. An option to consider is a wall-fitted head or plaque, which can give a discreet focus to an intimate enclosure.

became dominant during the last century and that was profoundly affected by writers such as Gertrude Jekyll and William Robinson. Before that time, whole gardens were composed of nothing other than paths, hedges, water and architectural and sculptural forms with very little planting. This is still a valid form of garden making, a balance between hard and soft surfaces, geometric and flowing shapes, caught in a play of light and shade.

By using ornaments, just as by using formally trained plants, it is possible to give the garden a structure for the entire year, even for the depths of winter. They evoke atmosphere and meditations – in our own age probably vaguer than in previous periods – such as references to the beautiful formal gardens of the past when we make use of classical statuary, or to the pleasures of pure form and shape when we place a contemporary piece in our garden. Whatever we choose and despite the fact that we are less familiar with the language of imagery than our ancestors were, the ornament will bring with it associations and memories that spring to mind whenever it is seen.

Sadly, many people have a mistaken idea as to what constitutes garden ornament but to judge from what is sold at garden centres that is hardly surprising. Some typical aberrations include concrete pigs, dogs and cats with inset green glass eyes and, also in concrete, Japanese ladies in kimonos.

Antique garden statuary and ornaments are sold regularly by the major auction houses and specialist dealers do exist. Such items can be expensive, although their cost is balanced by the fact that they are realizable assets. However, it is important to

1 These two attractively weathered pieces of stone, simply combined and set low in a shady corner of the garden with a tangled *Parthenocissus* creeper growing over them, have an undeniable, but melancholy, beauty.
2 Small geometric ornaments such as this obelisk and ball provide an ideal counterfoil to intricate leaf and flower shape and are appropriate to almost any style of architecture. This formal accent strikes an appropriate note in conjunction with the gravel path.
3 A pineapple is a much favoured ornamental shape, particularly popular in the eighteenth century when the fruit was a symbol of wealth and sophistication. Here, it provides an interesting contrast to the surrounding grasses, *Pulmonaria*, ferns, *Sedum*, *Acanthus* and Japanese anemones (*Anemone* × *hybrida*). Notice how it has been raised on a plinth.

1

2

3

remember that just because an ornament is old it does not necessarily follow that it is beautiful. Bad taste existed in the past too.

Most of us will have to be satisfied with reproductions of period garden ornaments. In fact, it is the traditional solution: garden statuary in the past was often just that, copies of famous antique statues. The two main sources are Italy and England. The Italians, through a long tradition, are better at statuary, while the English are better at producing good architectural ornaments, such as obelisks, columns, finials and urns. Both varieties are in forms of reconstituted stone. Beware, however: there are many exceedingly badly cast ornaments on the market, which are usually recognizable by the clumsy way dirt has been worked into cracks and joins to make pieces seem as though they have some age.

It is always good to commission work from artists and those with craft skills. If you do this, specify traditional materials – stone, bronze or lead or simulated versions of the two latter. A monumental mason, for instance, could execute an inscription in stone to attach to the garden wall.

Whatever you buy should be the best of its kind. It is better to have a fine large empty terracotta pot in the middle of the garden than to spend the same amount of money on a pretentious and badly cast reproduction statue. Of course, garden ornaments can be improvised but it calls for a sure eye. Really beautiful big stones, for example, can be arranged to form an entrancing tableau.

Choice will be dictated, too, by the style of your house and garden. It takes a house with classical detailing to accommodate a classical figure successfully just as it calls for a modern house to set off to advantage a contemporary sundial. It is the figurative ornaments which are more difficult to

1

place because they require a period context. That is why simple abstract geometric shapes are such a good solution. Pyramids, balls, cones, columns and pineapples go with virtually any architecture.

In a small garden it is unlikely that there will be room for more than one major ornament or at the most a pair. Too many small ornaments will result in a garden akin to a cemetery and diffuse and duplicate effect. The test of the correct placing of a garden ornament is whether, if it were removed, the whole picture would fall apart. It should create a focal point to which the eye is led. It could be placed at the end or centre of a vista, perhaps so that it could be enjoyed from the house during the winter. Well positioned in an enclosed garden room it might be a source of surprise and delight. If the ornament is to have any impact, it must be at least 4 feet (1.3 metres) in height, and be bold in silhouette so that it can be read at a distance.

1 A very beautiful weathered eighteenth-century stone sundial placed in the middle of a grassy walk breaks the monotony of the long path, which is flanked by herbaceous borders shown at their peak. The sundial has lost its plinth; its restoration would vastly improve both its appearance and proportions. A disadvantage of placing the sundial on the path is that the grass around its base has to be hand cut, but that is a small price to pay for such unstudied beauty.

2 A stone figure of the pilgrim St Rocco, in the baroque style, presides over a tiny knot garden. It is set into an alcove in a young box hedge, at the top of a small flight of steps to accentuate the importance of the figure. The scale of the figure – smaller than life – is exactly in proportion to the garden, in which not one of the clipped box spirals or domes is allowed to grow taller than the saint.

2

The longer the vista is, the bolder it needs to be.

Its importance can be emphasized by setting it on a mound, plinth or a platform with one or two steps up to it. It can also be highlighted by planting. An evergreen hedge cut into an arch, niche or apse makes an ideal setting for a garden statue; it can look equally handsome framed by some flowering climbers, for example, a Bourbon rose such as 'Kathleen Harrop' or 'Zéphirine Drouhin'. Most garden ornaments fall into one of two groups, those meant to be placed against a backdrop (statues and busts) and those which can be viewed from all four sides. Sundials should be free standing and open to the sun's rays.

It is often wise not to cement down the ornament until you are totally satisfied with the composition of the garden. And remember, the ornament is improved by weathering, a process that can be speeded up by the application of sour milk, yogurt or liquid manure.

1 This garlanded nymph seems to dance in her bower. However stunning the cascades of blossoms of the two roses, the rugosa 'Roseraie de l'Haÿ' and the climber 'American Pillar', the garden picture would be far less intriguing without the figure to draw the eye. The statue itself is a relatively crude Victorian one after an original by Canova, but it has weathered to perfection.
2 A bird bath at the end of this pretty path entices the visitor onwards. Between the series of arches laden with clematis are the receding lines of the borders full of sun-loving plants, and then a dark hornbeam that underlines the presence of the ornament. This is placed in front of a 'backcloth' of greenery and honeysuckle. Undoubtedly, the desire to traverse this path would be lessened without the ornament. There is added interest in the birdlife that it might attract.

1

SEATS

*T*o sit in a garden you have created is one of the greatest pleasures of all. From your seat you can contemplate your work in peace, feel the warmth of the sun, observe the play of light on the plants, and enjoy the fruits of your labour. From the seat, too, you notice what is wrong and make plans for action.

Something as basic as a seat seems so simple but, if it is permanently fixed, it can pose difficulties in terms of placing and setting. These problems, obviously, do not arise with movable seats, which are not part of the permanent composition of the garden; however, such seats do require storage space when not in use. I feel this type of seating should not draw attention to itself, either by its design or, above all, by the fabrics used for its upholstery. And what looks right in the south of France or in Australia beneath strong sunlight looks regrettably offkey under greyer skies. Remember that garden furniture should be discreet, even self-effacing, and should in no way compete with the world of nature. Virulently patterned fabrics have no place within the perimeters of a small garden. In the same way that containers are dotted around in summer with plantings complementary to the basic design framework, so garden furniture should takes its place. Too often it is of a vulgarity that any normal person would instantly reject for any room within the house. The same principles apply outside as in.

In a small garden it is unlikely that there is space for more than one permanent seat. Its siting must be part of the basic planning of the garden and the first consideration will be whether you want to sit in

This seat, placed on a paving of setts, is enclosed on three sides
by raised flowerbeds contained by railway sleepers.
Behind, there is a tall screen of evergreens for privacy
and protection from the wind. The seat is simply made, of
lengths of wood supported by four short wooden poles.
It is a seat that was clearly designed for resting on a walk
around the garden rather than for prolonged occupation. The
delightful mixture of plants surrounding the seat
includes ivy, geraniums, potentillas, bergenias,
a dwarf pine and foxgloves.

A

A A stone bench needs an unfussy setting. The more exposed the garden, the more important it is to create

sheltered corners. A dense hedge of yew (*Taxus baccata*) holds this bench in a sober protective embrace.

B

B In spring and in autumn more than at other times of the year you want to be able to take full advantage of any brief bursts of

sunshine. A wheelbarrow seat is a wonderful extravagance that can be used to follow the sun around the garden.

C

C A solid teak garden seat is one of the best and most readily available pieces of traditional garden furniture. It blends well

with brick, stone, gravel and plants and seems to be at its most welcoming when set against a warm wall.

sun or shade. A seat can be tucked away in a sheltered corner but it can also be sited to take advantage of the garden's greatest spectacle.

Generally, to be in use the whole year a seat requires shelter and that indicates that it must be set against a wall or hedge. If shade is wanted, barriers such as walls and hedges can help create it but a more effective solution is to place a seat within an arbour, even the simplest kind made of trellis. Remember it is always better for a permanent seat to be set on a hard surface. Otherwise, the seat has to be moved for the mower or the grass underneath has to be hand clipped. Unpaved ground beneath a seat will get muddy in wet weather, as can any unpaved path leading to it.

A seat provides an opportunity for enjoying scent, one of the delights of the garden that is often neglected. You can surround the seat with a sweet-smelling honeysuckle, such as *Lonicera japonica halliana,* or place it close to the astringent aroma of cotton lavender. Whatever your preference, try always to think of scented plants as essential partners of the garden seat. Just to have rosemary within reach to press between the fingers will give pleasure twelve months of the year.

With ingenuity almost anything can be turned into a garden seat, from a section of a tree trunk to a railway sleeper or a plank of wood supported by brick piers. But most of us will look to what is

1 A nineteenth-century antique iron bench with a wooden seat has been placed on an area of stone paving. The back is composed of a beautifully orchestrated pattern of fern leaves. Such a seat would be a costly investment but would give lasting pleasure. It is painted dark green and set against a background of variegated laurel (**Aucuba japonica**).
2 This handsome wooden garden armchair in the grand style of the eighteenth century has a lattice back and decorative profiling along the top. It has been placed in a sunny spot for the summer against a reddish-grey brick wall, which goes well with its blue-grey colour. The two box pyramids that flank the seat will be perfect companions when fully grown.
3 A bench and folding chairs provide inexpensive seating for a stripped Victorian pinewood table used for alfresco eating. They are sited in an enclosure of leaf and blossom that is reinforced by terracotta pots containing pale violet pansies. The flowering plants, which are in magenta and blue tones, include borage, **Campanula poscharskyana** and **Gladiolus byzantinus**. An old knotty rosemary bush adds a heady fragrance to this dining area.

1

2

3

1 The placing of an arch of honeysuckle over this simple bench on the edge of an old-fashioned garden is a master touch. The support is a very basic structure yet the result is completely enchanting. The top of the grassy bank behind the bench is marked by a fine lattice-work fence edging a pergola of pleached limes.

1

2 An old stripped pine bench, table and chairs furnish a charming garden alcove that is paved with old bricks. Shelter and support for the simple pergola of larch poles is provided by the brick wall. The raised bed next to the wall is planted with hostas and the whole has been encompassed by a purple-leaved vine and a pink rose that is just about to burst into bloom.

commercially available. Of the materials, plastic is totally unsympathetic. Iron, stone and reconstituted stone are undoubtedly the most durable, although iron requires periodic re-painting to keep rust at bay. Wooden seats can look very handsome, but, other than those made of plain teak, most will require sanding and re-staining or re-painting every few years to avoid rotting. If you want them to last for some time, they really need to be placed under cover during the winter months.

As in the case of ornaments and containers, let your choice of seat relate to the overall style of the house and garden. In a small area, seats can draw too much attention to themselves, their size or their colour making them too conspicuous. Both points need careful consideration. Usually, no more than two or three people will ever sit together on a seat, so there is no point in acquiring an out-of-scale monster. In the case of colour, white tends to be too bright and dominating; instead, to achieve a more harmonious effect, it is sensible to stick to off-whites, greys and dark greens.

When it comes to style, clashes as violent as a rustic seat in a formal town garden or a reproduction Chippendale in a cottage garden should be avoided at all costs. Fortunately, some seats are classics and seem right for any setting – for instance, the plain teak bench with back and arms will fit anywhere and has so far defied vulgarization. Benches made of stone or reconstituted stone hardly ever look out of place.

Antique iron and stone seats can be purchased, at a price, from specialist dealers or in sales. Luckily, a large range of reproduction seats is now available. These include items as varied as Victorian park benches with marvellous decorated ends and seats of lacy Regency Gothic tracery. An interesting revival is the single garden seat, which is ideal for placing in a quiet spot.

Do, however, think carefully what you require of your garden seat before you purchase it. In the main, portable, upholstered furniture is for lounging on, and, accordingly, should be chosen for comfort as well as good looks and practicality. Heavier, permanent seating, on the other hand, is usually for short, contemplative pauses; if it is for more than that, make sure the seat is really comfortable and will take cushions or squabs. If the intention is to eat at a table, make sure that the seat is high enough. It is all too easy to be seduced by appearances into buying an expensive mistake.

2

CONTAINERS

*P*lants in containers can be a constant source of delight, bringing colour and life to the garden at all times of the year. They can be treated in a formal manner – being arranged, for example, in symmetrical groups – and in an informal way, being used more sparingly with, for instance, a flowering plant shown to advantage against a background of foliage. Potted plants can be used as points of emphasis and, when they are strategically positioned, make a few flowers seem many. For those with only a paved area or rooftop from which to make a garden they alone make the exercise at all possible.

Containers come in much the same materials as garden ornaments, with several additions. Stone, as always, is the most beautiful as well as the most expensive. An alternative is reconstituted stone, usually in the form of reproductions of period containers, but these need to weather and obtain a patina before they look their best. Terracotta and earthenware are sympathetic materials although, being porous, they are subject to damage by frost in winter unless kept dry. When the winter is severe it may be prudent to take them in. There are earthenware pots with ceramic glazes, often in blue and white, the less sturdy of which definitely need winter shelter. They can be very lovely, striking an original and exotic note dotted around the garden. Although wooden containers are subject to decay, the half-barrel and the square painted Versailles tub, available in various sizes, remain garden classics. The latter is now available in fibreglass and it requires a very sharp eye indeed to spot that it is not of wood. The same process of reproduction has successfully been applied to

A glorious midsummer display of pink, white and red pelargoniums growing in hanging baskets and window boxes on the first-floor back verandah of a town house. Looking out from the house, the foliage and flowers make a charming screen through which to view the garden proper. Containers enable plants to be grown almost anywhere as long as there is enough suitable light. However, potted plants do require constant attention, and judging and maintaining the right supply of water can be a problem, but the rewards are self-evident.

period lead cisterns and urns. Containers made of concrete should be treated with caution but there are examples of contemporary design that go well with today's architecture. Wire hanging baskets should not be forgotten if you can cope with the difficulty of watering. One material, plastic, should not be used if it is going to be seen. Its hard shiny surface is out of place in the world of nature.

There is a huge range of shapes and sizes of plant containers, from the simple earthenware crock to the elaborate fluted urn. The style of the garden and house and where the container is to be sited will be important considerations when choosing, but always take care to match the pot to the plant. A plant needs adequate root space and good drainage; a plant must appear stable as well as being so – there is little worse than a plant which looks as though the wind could blow it over. As well as its size and shape, think about its colour, and its habit – trailing plants need pots of adequate height to show themselves to good effect, and it would be a shame to obscure the decorative details of a container with comparatively dull foliage.

Stick to classic shapes. Reconstituted stone urns, jardinières and troughs reproduce classics from the gardens of previous centuries. They have stood the test of time and have never been bettered. Avoid inferior badly cast containers in concrete which have been artificially aged. Well-cast terra-cotta pots also exist in classic styles with lions' masks, swags and other simple motifs on them. Sadly, these too are often badly made.

Containers in the garden fall into two groups, the movable and immovable. Those that are large and difficult to move, such as a tall classical urn on a pedestal, really rank as garden ornaments and should be treated as such. And, whatever their size, the nature of the materials they are made of mean *2* that containers of stone, reconstituted stone and concrete are a permanent part of the garden scene and need to be carefully sited.

The same uses can be applied to the movable ones but they, in fact, fulfil a far wider brief, from embellishing steps to flanking arches. They can be part of the garden picture for the whole of the year, particularly if planted with evergreens such as clipped box, and, more than anything else, they enable the dullest of gardens to be enlivened with instant bloom and foliage. Because they are movable, it is possible to ring the changes throughout the year. The area nearest the house is the ideal

1 Simple ornament is often more effective than confused detail – a principle embraced instinctively in hotter climates. Here, five beautiful large antique earthenware containers with a green glaze carry a permanent planting of grey-leaved *Senecio* and evergreen shrubs. This group softens the plain lines of the Mediterranean architecture and the hardness of the stone paving inset with a pebble circle in a perfectly balanced composition. Glazed pots such as these, which are not frost proof, need to be taken indoors during the cold months.

2 Half-barrel casks make handsome containers for plants. Part of their attraction lies in the perfect proportions, and the combination of materials – weathered wood circled with iron hoops. They are particularly useful for tall-growing plants, including shrubs, standard fuchsias and lilies. This group of tubs is placed in the middle of a brick-paved area to make a pretty seasonal display of pink and blue flowers and soft green foliage. The tubs contain a summer planting of tall spider flowers (*Cleome* 'Hassieriana') at the centre, giving height, and beneath them there is an attractive mixed underplanting that includes both petunias and verbena.

1

2

3

place for containers, bringing to life a part of the garden much used in the summer months and also handy for the constant watering potted plants demand. Of course, movable containers need to be planted and placed with discretion. Scattered around without due consideration they can disfigure rather than enhance a garden.

There is no doubt about it, containers are hard work, albeit of a most rewarding kind. Succulent plants such as sedums are about the only plants that can be left untouched and unwatered to fend for themselves and successfully increase and multiply, cascading over the edges. Almost all plants grown in containers demand periodic soil changing, feeding and watering; if these chores are neglected, plants will die. Give plants the preparation and soil they require – for example, with lime-hating plants such as rhododendrons, the compost must be lime free, while alpines need good drainage. And make sure the plant is suitable for the site chosen for the pot – some plants need full sun, others part shade.

Containers can take permanent plants. Box, for instance, is fairly tolerant of drought and offers enormous possibilities in the form of box spirals, cones and balls. Bay trees, either pyramid or standard, look very handsome when grown in Versailles tubs. The reliable *Viburnum tinus* can be container grown and so can holly and Portugal laurel (*Prunus lusitanica*), which can be clipped into a neat dome. And then there are deciduous shrubs, including maples (species and cultivars of *Acer*) and the perennial flowering plants of marginal hardiness such as agapanthus, with their

1 Single containers can be given added importance by positioning them on a raised surface such as the coping of a balustrade, as here, or on a wall. This superb terracotta basket is filled for the summer with a strongly coloured centre planting of a red fuchsia and a purple heliotrope surrounded by trailing pink pelargoniums.
2 Steps provide an opportunity to display plants to advantage on a variety of levels, but they must be wide enough so the plants do not get in the way. A double row of fuchsias and begonias in pots makes a magnificent show, lining both sides of steps that lead down to a terrace. Notice the two standard fuchsias flanking the bottom.
3 A modest group of earthenware pots containing geraniums and petunias brings much-needed summer colour to a paved garden. Potted plants are a very good way of enlivening paved areas such as this.

A

A Versailles tubs, square wooden containers, go particularly well with clipped bay (*Laurus nobilis*). They fit in with architecture – it is not by chance that they are often seen flanking French doors – and rather formal furniture.

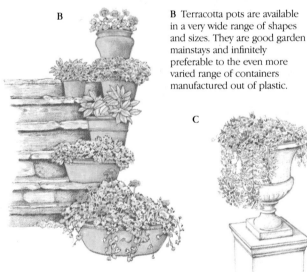

B

B Terracotta pots are available in a very wide range of shapes and sizes. They are good garden mainstays and infinitely preferable to the even more varied range of containers manufactured out of plastic.

C

C An urn, it has been said, is as good as its pedestal. Certainly the two need to be in proportion and carefully positioned to make the most of a tall container. The height of this urn allows for the trailing growth of the unusual plant, *Lotus berthelotii.*

1

2

1 The introduction of a pair of Chinese blue and white containers for the summer months at the entrance to this predominantly green garden strikes an original note. Glazed containers of this kind were much in use in the eighteenth century and it is a fashion well worth reviving. I would have preferred a bolder planting, though – tall white *Lilium regale* would have been much more impressive.

2 A single urn filled with white daisy-like marguerites (*Chrysanthemum frutescens*) makes an effective focal point to an area of paved brick. The detailed ornamentation of the urn is counterbalanced by the simplicity of the setting and of the planting. The geraniums at the base of the urn are particularly good plants for foliage and ground cover.

3 Hydrangeas in bloom, with their wonderful large frothy flowerheads, make spectacular container plants. Another advantage is their long flowering period. The mophead hydrangea (*H. macrophylla*) comes in a huge range of varieties and colours, from metallic purple through every shade of blue to pure white.

pretty heads of blue flowers. Best of all are orange and lemon trees, the classic ingredient of the great Italian gardens, but they are tender and if they are to survive they must be moved inside during the winter months.

The possibilities for seasonal planting are huge. I always aim at two plantings: a spring and a summer one, aided by a few permanent features such as trailing ivy or evergreens to maintain interest between the flowering periods. Even in the darkest months there is scope for winter-flowering pansies, some of the very early bulbs (for example, dwarf irises) and heather (which can be treated as a permanent planting).

Even very accomplished gardeners often make the mistake of having too many small containers. The visual effect is restless and spotty. Rather than, cluttering the garden with many little containers, it is far better to have a few large ones that are well maintained and strikingly planted.

A selection of plants suitable for growing in containers is given in Lists 14–17 on pages 140–41.

GARDEN BUILDINGS

*T*he great gardens of the past were frequently adorned with every type of building, from temples in the classical style to rocky grottos, from pagodas to hermits' cells. One purpose of these buildings was to evoke in the mind of the visitor, in the same way that ornaments might, a whole series of thoughts and images, from the vanished glories and gods of the ancient world to the mysteries and wonders of the Orient. At the same time, they had the practical purpose of providing shade from the hot sun and shelter from unexpected showers. Similar considerations ought to be applicable to buildings in a small modern garden. We should still aim to combine imagination and fantasy with practical use.

Garden buildings, as in the past, are an opportunity for light-hearted architecture making abundant use of motifs from other periods and countries and, above all, drawing on the repertory of ornament. They need to be well designed and attractive to the eye at all times of the year. Nothing, however, is more deadening than most of the mass-manufactured garden houses available today, little more than unattractive timber shacks devoid of any architectural design concept. Fortunately, there are now some specialist manufacturers who do produce a variety of pretty summerhouses and gazebos.

In a small garden, a building of this kind usually makes the need for another ornament unnecessary. Its siting will be determined by the desire for sun or shade and the overall design of the garden. It could be either a focal point or tucked away for peace and privacy in a quiet corner. Such a building can be enhanced by the trick of setting it

A generous scale and a bold interesting outline are two essential ingredients of a successful garden building. Even in a small garden, a building can make a splendid focal point, as here, and provide shelter from sun and rain and a seat from which to enjoy the vista or relax in quiet contemplation. This octagonal summerhouse has been embellished with a Gothic arch that is inset into a framework of painted trellis. A golden hop (*Humulus lupulus* 'Aureus') rambles up the building, and a pagoda-like tiled roof completes the exotic composition.

A To find a simple ready-made summerhouse that is well built and attractively designed is very difficult. For my own garden I chose something less than a summerhouse, a neat cabin-like Gothic seat very like the one set in this elegant tableau.

B If you have the necessary skills, it may be worth designing and erecting your own garden building. Bear in mind that anything close to the house should follow its style of architecture. A pretty, rustic structure, such as this, is probably best some distance from the house.

1

on a platform or at the top of a short flight of steps. It can be further embroidered with planting, above all of scented climbers.

It is far better not to have a garden building than to have an ugly one. A really beautiful seat may be a better option. A tool or potting shed is certainly useful but it is always a deadening feature. It should always be tucked away and screened from sight. The garden proper should only provide a setting for a building which adds to its beauty.

The mood you want to create will, to a large degree, dictate the form such a building will take. Its proposed use and the budget available are other considerations. In the main it will be a place of repose during the summer with a seat from which to enjoy the fruits of your labours. But if space and finance permit, the construction of a work room away from the house has its attractions. This would be less of an indulgence if lighting and heating were installed so it could be used all year.

2

The most important consideration in erecting a garden building is scale, both in relation to the garden and to the house. The general fault is to make garden buildings too small and apologetic. When the scale is wrong the result will be awkward and unhappy. The proportions are of vital importance, too; badly proportioned windows, usually on the small side, are among the main reasons why many commercially available buildings are so ugly. Next to scale and proportion I would place silhouette, for the outline of the building will be seen at a distance against a background of shrubs, trees and sky.

The greatest enemy to putting up a successful garden building is timidity. More even than the house, a garden building, because it is a flight of fancy, is an expression of the owner's personality. When it works, it can give a garden a uniqueness and individuality which, today, are all too often sadly absent from most gardens.

1 A workroom away from the house can make a delightful garden building. Here, a library and writing room, built in the painted clapboard style of New England architecture, opens out on to a charming little formal garden. Its sharply pitched roof lifts it out of the ordinary; notice how the shape has been repeated in the clipped pyramids of box. Although this would be an expensive project, since it needs electricity for lighting and heating, the cost can be balanced against the gain of a room which can be used for all twelve months of the year.

2 A small, elegant summerhouse facing the French windows of a town house makes an agreeable place in which to sit and eat. It is the central feature of a charming garden, surrounded by luxuriant planting and wide paths. The fact that the path does not lead to it directly in a straight line makes this little garden seem just that much bigger than it really is.

WATER

Water has been part of garden design since antiquity. The principles of hydraulics were re-discovered during the Renaissance and taken to heart. Soon no garden was complete without some form of water device: fountains with huge jets soaring into the air, grottos with trick mechanical water effects which soaked the unwary visitor, vast cascades, artificial ponds and rivers, water staircases, even hydraulic organs playing music. Notable examples of this grand tradition can still be seen at Versailles and at Hellbrun Castle, Salzburg. Although we are dealing with small domestic spaces, there is scope for the imaginative use of water in gardens.

The response when seeing a lake, pond, rivulet, waterfall or fountain is one of wonder and sheer delight. When still, water evokes tranquillity. But, when moving, it can bring a shimmering sparkle that animates the entire garden scene. Just the sound of running water produces a sense of calm satisfaction on a hot summer's day.

That said, making water a feature of the garden is not without problems and disadvantages. The most serious, of course, is the fact that even very shallow water is deep enough to drown a young child; this can rule out most forms of water in the garden while your children are small. Water can present other daunting and recurring problems, too. A pond can be subject to flooding through rain and snow, and, if it freezes, any plant and animal life may be destroyed and the structure may suffer damage. Fish, which are always at risk from marauding cats and predatory birds, can be poisoned if the water is fouled by garden debris – a pond should not be positioned

The tranquil reflective qualities of water have been used to great
advantage in a square pool placed formally at the
centre of a short brick path that is lined with dwarf box
hedges and flanked at one end by box balls and at the other
by standard bay trees. Instead of the pool being edged in brick
or stone, weathered wooden planks are used. The surrounding
planting of hostas, lady's mantle (*Alchemilla mollis*) and
bergenias softens the straight lines, while water lilies
break up the mirror-like surface of the water.

A

A In a garden where formal and architectural features dominate, an informal pool lavishly planted with moisture-loving plants is quite out of place. The intended 'naturalness' of some rigid pool liners is conspicuously unsuccessful whatever the setting. Use the geometric shape of the pool to reinforce the formality of the garden. The installation of a jet will add the pleasure of the sight and sound of moving water.

B

B In the small garden a centrally positioned pool can take up space that might be better used as an area for sitting and dining or for planting – the best position for a pool is in full sun, a position where you might well choose to give people and plants priority. A wall fountain is a good alternative to a pool.

under trees but even if it is not it may collect fallen leaves. During hot summer weather, when ponds attract mosquitoes and other insects, keeping water from becoming stagnant and smelly can be difficult, especially if it is still.

The attractions, however, are undeniable and, for the dedicated gardener, they will always far outweigh the problems. These days, many of the construction and plumbing problems have been greatly reduced. It is a relatively simple matter to build an acceptable pool using pre-formed fibreglass shapes or flexible liners and for the amateur the result will be more reliable than something built of concrete. It is easy to keep the water aerated using a submersible electric recycling pump, which is cheap to operate and can be used to feed a simple jet or fountain.

The central design problem in a small garden is that any use of water is so patently artificial. That is why 'natural' pools on a small scale always look so ludicrous; it is like attempting to create a woodland dell in a small rectangular garden – it is so obviously phoney. Unfortunately, the very worst designs of fibreglass pools, those with irregular outlines, have become a commonplace of suburban gardening. The most successful uses of water in a small garden result from accepting, and often emphasizing, that very artificiality by containing the water within a clearly defined structure.

In a small space a formal pond should be the focal point of the whole garden, perhaps placed at the centre away from the shade of trees so that it reflects as much of the sky as possible. Simple geometric shapes – not irregular ones – are best. The pond can be sunk into the ground, its shape emphasized by paving that frames the water and conceals the waterline. A formal pond can equally be made as a raised basin with a parapet of stone or brick enclosing it, a feature not only pleasant to sit on to contemplate reflections but useful for displaying containers to advantage in the summer.

Two iron spouts, one above the other, feed water into brick troughs, the lower one of which extends under a bridge of thick wood planks, with abundant planting on either side. This is an arrangement of the utmost simplicity which is skilfully built and incorporates the refreshing sounds of running water. The varied planting includes herbs and vegetables and moisture-loving plants such as yellow marsh marigolds (*Caltha palustris*), the feathery, dark red astilbe 'Fanal' and the white margined leaves of *Hosta crispula*.

A pond must always be of sufficient size to balance the garden's composition. Anything less than about 8 feet (2.7 metres) in diameter will look like an over-dressed puddle, and it will also need to be about 3 feet (1 metre) deep. If you want to plant marginals, plants that like their feet in water such as some irises, the pond will need a shallower area near the rim – between 6 inches and 1 foot (15 and 30 centimetres) deep. A geometric sheet of still water reflecting the sky and bearing water lilies (*Nymphaea*) is quite beautiful but to get the best effect not more than one-third of the surface should be covered by lily pads. The other choice – jets of water propelled by an electric recycling pump – provides sound and movement. Whatever the decision, remember that any type of pond will need to be emptied of water and thoroughly cleaned out every three years.

Small fountains incorporating sculpture can look wonderful as focal points in gardens. However, the scale and siting of these ornaments must be considered with the same discrimination you would apply to other decorative features. My own preference, though, in a very small garden would always be for a wall fountain. This brings all the pleasures of water in miniature. A wall fountain can be as simple as a metal spout or as elaborate as a dolphin or lion's head mask. The tableau which can be built around it can also be as complex or as simple as you wish. The depth and shape of the basin and the fall of the jet allow for many variations. If there is deep moist soil at the foot of the fountain, you can create a lush effect by planting hostas, some of the irises (*Iris sibirica* and *I. laevigata*, for instance) and arum lilies (*Zantedeschia aethiopica*).

These relatively conventional uses of water in the garden, themselves so capable of interesting treatment, far from exhaust the possibilities. Some spectacularly successful small gardens have been created by excavating almost the whole site and filling it with water, walkways being provided in the form of decking. The result can be breathtaking but unfortunately the expense could be too. At the other extreme, a simple but very attractive use of water is to have a low jet splashing over a bed of large pebbles – or an interesting stone shape bedded in pebbles – either of which will produce a pleasing effect of sound and movement without creating the risks to children that even the smallest, shallowest stretch of water can present.

2

1 A secret fountain in a secret corner of the garden – imagine the delight of coming upon this on a hot summer's day. Fountains can be used to great effect in a small space. Fine jets of water from the statue splash down into a small basin and then overflow to the circular pond below. The proportions of the fountain – the height of the statue and pedestal, and the diameters of the basin and pond – are beautifully calculated and the moving water dappled by sunlight gives a feeling of refreshment.

2 A simple but telling arrangement in which water spills from one metal gully into another and then on in an artificial rivulet through grass and a lush carpet of baby's tears (*Helxine soleirolii*). The restrained planting includes a vigorous clump of bamboo.

3 This single low plume of water erupting from the centre of the generous-sized circular stone has a vaguely Japanese look to it. The whole is set in a bed of large pale cobble stones – a much safer way of introducing water into a garden used by small children than a pool. A fountain such as this would be extremely appropriate in the paved garden of a very modern house.

3

PLANTING SUGGESTIONS

Symbols and abbreviations

○	sunny	*Miscellaneous*	
◑	tolerates light shade	c	culinary
●	tolerates full shade	cvs	cultivars (horticultural
Soil			varieties)
A	needs acid soil	d	dessert
D	dry, well-drained soil	decid.	deciduous
L	needs or will tolerate	evg.	evergreen
	chalky soil	fls	flowers
M	moist, water-retentive but at	fr.	fruit
	the same time reasonably	frag.	fragrant
	well-drained	h.	hardy*
S	standard soil which is	herb.	herbaceous
	reasonably humus rich and	lge	large
	well drained	lvs	leaves
Season		per.	perennial
e.	early	sm.	small
m.	mid	v.	very
l.	late	z.	zone

* The term 'not fully hardy' signifies that the subject may need winter protection according to the climate it is in; plants in pots are always more vulnerable. Where applicable hardiness zone ratings for the US are given (eg. z.7).

1 PLANTS TO COMBINE WITH PAVING

Ajuga reptans 'Multicolor'	◑ S; 4–12in (10–30cm), mat to 1ft (30cm); evg. per.; fls blue, m. spring to summer; lvs green with bronze, yellow, pink.
Alchemilla mollis	● S; 18in (45cm); herb. per.; fls yellow-green, m. summer; lvs broadly lobed; easy to please.
Armeria maritima	○ D; 6–12in (15–30cm), mat to 1ft (30cm); evg. per.; fls white to blood-red; lvs linear.
Anthemis nobilis	○ S; 8in (20cm), mat to 18in (45cm); per.; fls daisy-like; lvs aromatic; (also *A.n.* 'Plena', yellow pompon flowers).
Campanula carpatica	○ D (L); 12in (30cm), spread to 16in (40cm); herb. per.; fls white to purple.
Dianthus alpinus	○ D (L); 4in (10cm), mat to 1ft (30cm); evg. per.; fls pink.
Dianthus cvs	○ D (L); 6–12in (15–30cm), mat to 18in (45cm); evg. per.; lvs grey; fls white to carmine.
Euphorbia myrsinites	○ D; 18in (45cm), prostrate to 2ft (60cm); evg. per.; lvs grey; fls lime yellow.
Sedum acre 'Aureum'	○ D; 2in (5cm), mat to 1ft (30cm); per.; lvs yellow.
Sempervivum tectorum	○ D; 6in (15cm), rosettes to 1ft (30cm); evg. per.; lvs dark green, tipped brown; fls pink to purplish red.
Thymus praecox	○ D (L); 1in (2½cm), mat to 2ft (60cm); evg. per.; fls purple m. summer.

2 FLOWERING CLIMBERS AND WALL SHRUBS

Ceanothus 'Gloire de Versailles'	○ S; 6ft (2m); decid.; fls powder-blue, e. summer; z. 7.
Chaenomeles speciosa	○ S; 6ft (2m); decid.; fls scarlet, m. spring; fr. yellow autumn; z. 5.
Clematis macropetala	◑ S; 9ft (3m); decid.; fls nodding, single, lavender-blue, l. spring; z. 5–6.
Clematis viticella	◑ S; 12ft (4m); decid.; fls reddish to purple blue, m. summer to e. autumn; z. 6.
Cytisus battandieri	○ S; 12ft (4m); decid. or semi-evg.; fls yellow, attractive pineapple scent, e. summer; lvs grey silky; z.9.
Hydrangea petiolaris	◑ M; 45ft (15m); decid.; self-clinging; fls white, e. summer; z. 6.
Ipomoea purpurea	○ S; 9ft (3m); annual; fls blue, l. summer; sow seed in spring.
Jasminum nudiflorum	● S; 16ft (2m); decid.; fls yellow, l. winter; z. 6.
Jasminum polyanthum	○ S; 9ft (3m); decid.; fls white, fragrant, l. summer; z. 9.
Lathyrus latifolius	○ S; 9ft (3m); herb. per.; fls rose-purple to white, l. summer.
Magnolia grandiflora	○ M (l); 30ft (10m); evg.; fls white, frag., m. summer; needs warm wall; z. 7b–1c.
Schizophragma hydrangeoides	○ M; 30ft (10m); decid.; self-clinging; fls white, m. summer; z. 5.
Solanum crispum 'Glasnevin'	○ S; 12ft (4m); decid.; fls mauve and yellow, m. summer to m. autumn; not fully h.; z. 9.
Tropaeolum speciosum	◑ D; 6ft (2m); herb. per.; fls red, m. summer.

3 CLIMBERS AND WALL SHRUBS FOR FOLIAGE AND BERRIES

Actinidia kolomikta	○ S; 20ft (7m); lvs green, pink and white; fls white, frag., m. summer; z. 5.
Ampelopsis brevipedunculata	○ S; 12ft (4m); decid.; fr. china-blue, turning purple m. autumn; not fully h.; z. 5b.
Cotoneaster horizontalis	◑ D; 3ft (1m); to 10ft (3m) wide; decid.; lvs sm.; fr. red l. summer; fls white; z. 6.
Hedera canariensis 'Gloire de Marengo'	◑ S; 6ft (2m); lvs grey-green, irregular creamy margin; not fully h.; z. 8.
Hedera helix 'Goldheart'	◑ S; 9ft (3m); lvs dark green with central yellow blotch; z. 7.
Parthenocissus tricuspidata	◑ M; 45ft (15m); decid.; lvs crimson in autumn; fr. dark blue, waxy; z. 5.
Pyracantha coccinea 'Lalandei'	○ S; 15ft (5m); decid.; fr. orange; fls white corymbs; spiny; z. 7.
Rosa 'Cupid'	○ S; 15ft (5m); hips large, orange-red, persistent, e. autumn; fls light pink.
Vitis 'Brant'	◑ M; 15ft (5m); lvs deeply lobed, red to purple, veined yellow in m. autumn; fr. small, black; z. 5.
Vitis vinifera 'Purpurea'	◑ M; 15ft (5m); lvs claret red, ageing to red-purple; fr. black; z. 5b.

4 CLIMBING ROSES

All deciduous and US zones 6–7 unless stated.

'Aloha'	○ S; 5–10ft (1.5–3m); fls double, pink, frag. recurrent e. summer to e. autumn; mildew resistant; good pillar.
'Climbing Allgold'	○ S; 8ft (2.4m); fls semi-double, golden yellow, recurrent m. summer to e. autumn.
'Constance Spry'	○ S; 8ft (2.4m); fls lge pink, frag., e. summer
'Dorothy Perkins'	○ S; 10ft (3.3m); fls bright pink, e. summer; mildew prone, unsuited for walls.

'Gloire de Dijon'	○ S; 10ft (3.3m); fls buff-orange, double, recurrent, m. summer to m. autumn.
'Golden Showers'	○ S; 6–10ft (2–3.3m); fls numerous, lge, double yellow, m. summer to e. autumn.
'Helen Knight'	○ S; 7ft (2.1m); fls single, clear yellow, lightly frag., e. summer; lvs dainty; stems dark.
'Kathleen Harrop'	○ S; 8ft (2.4m); fls shell-pink, recurrent e. summer to e. autumn.
'Maigold'	○ S; 8–12ft (2.4m); fls semi-double, yellow, frag., m. summer; lvs lge, dark green; v. thorny.
'Parkdirektor Riggers'	○ S; 12ft (4m); fls semi-double, lge clusters, red, recurrent m. summer to e. autumn; lvs dark green.
'Paul's Scarlet Climber'	○ S; 10ft (3.3m); fls semi-double in small clusters, crimson, m. summer.
'Raubritter'	○ S; 8ft (2.4m); fls numerous, semi-double, pompon-like, purplish-pink, m. summer.
'Réveil Dijonnais'	○ S; 8ft (2.4m); fls numerous, semi-double, lge, scarlet-crimson, yellow centred, recurrent m. summer to e. autumn.
'Souvenir de la Malmaison'	○ S; 10ft (3.3m); fls lge, pale pink, frag., recurrent m. summer to e. autumn.
'The New Dawn'	○ S; 12ft (4m); fls semi-double, pink, in clusters, m. summer; lvs glossy.
'Zéphirine Drouhin'	○ S; 9ft (3m); fls semi-double, cerise-carmine, frag., e. or m. summer; dead head.

5   ROCK PLANTS FOR WALLS

Alyssum saxatile 'Citrinum'	○ S; 8in (20cm); mat to 18in (45cm); fls pale yellow; lvs grey.
Androsace sarmentosa	◑ S; 6in (15cm); mat to 2ft (60cm), fls pink, spring; protect from winter wet.
Anthemis cupaniana	○ D; 6in (15cm); cushion 1ft (30cm) wide; fls daisy-like summer to autumn; lvs grey, feathery.
Arabis ferdinandi-coburghii	○ S; 6in (15cm); cushion 1ft (30cm) wide; evg. per.; white, m. spring (also *A. f.-c.* 'Variegata', lvs variegated).
Aubrieta deltoidea	◑ S; 6in (15cm); cushion or hanging to 2ft (60cm); evg. per.; fls purple range, m. spring.
Campanula poscharskyana	◑ D (L); 6in (15cm); 2ft (60cm) spread; evg. per.; fls purple-blue, l. spring to l. summer.
Cerastium tomentosum	○ S; 6in (15cm); mat to 18in (45cm), evg. per.; fls white, m. spring; lvs grey.
Cheiranthus 'Harpur Crewe'	○ S; 10in (25cm); evg. per.; fls double, yellow.
Helianthemum nummularium	○ D (L); 6in (15cm); mat to 2ft (60 cm), evg. per.; fls yellow, l. spring, some cream, white, pink, orange.
Iberis sempervirens	○ S; 8in (20cm); semi-prostrate to 30in (75cm); evg. per.; fls white, m. spring to m. summer.
Phlox subulata	○ M (L); 6in (15cm); mat to 3ft (1m), per.; fls pink to purple, l. spring.
Saxifraga longifolia	○ S; 1–2ft (30–60cm); evg. per.; lvs rosettes; fls white on long stems m. summer; protect from winter wet.

6   EVERGREEN HEDGES

Buxus sempervirens	◑ D; 9ft (3m); lvs sm., round; prune summer; also for topiary and container foliage; z. 6.
Buxus sempervirens 'Suffruticosa'	◑ D; 1ft (30cm); prune spring and summer; good for edging; z. 6.
Cupressus macrocarpa	○ S; 12ft (4m); conifer; lvs aromatic when crushed; trim in m. autumn; z. 8.

Elaeagnus pungens 'Maculata'	◑ S; 9ft (3m); lvs centre yellow; secateur clip spring; z. 7.
Ilex × altaclerensis 'Golden King'	◑ S; 9ft (3m); lvs yellow margined, few spines; fr. red; secateur clip autumn; z. 7.
Ilex aquifolium	◑ S; 12ft (4m); lvs dark green, spiny; fr. red; secateur clip l. autumn; z. 7.
Ligustrum ovalifolium 'Aureum'	◑ S; 12ft (4m); lvs sm., yellow; prune spring and summer; z. 6.
Lonicera nitida	○ S; 4ft (1.2m); lvs minute; good narrow hedge; prune in e. spring; z. 7.
Prunus laurocerasus	◑ S; 12ft (4m); lvs lge, apple green; clip in m. summer; z. 7.
Prunus lusitanica	○ S; 18ft (6m); lvs dark green; secateur clip in spring; z. 7.
Rosmarinus officinalis 'Miss Jessup's Upright'	○ D; 5ft (1.5m); lvs narrow grey-green; fl. blue, summer; erect habit; not fully h.; z. 7–8.
Santolina chamaecyparissus	○ D; 2–3ft (40–60cm); lvs narrow grey; shear before yellow fls in l. spring; z.7.
Taxus baccata	◑ S; 9ft (3m); lvs sm., dark green; fr. red; trim spring or autumn; z. 7.
Taxus × intermedia 'Hicksii'	◑ S; 9ft (3m); lvs larger than above, makes more uniform hedge; z. 5.
Thuja plicata	○ S; 12ft (4m); lvs aromatic; slow growing; trim in spring; z. 5.
Viburnum tinus	● D; 6ft (2m); fls white to pink l. autumn to e. spring; fr. blue-black, l. summer to e. autumn; z. 7.

7   DECIDUOUS HEDGES

Berberis thunbergii 'Rose Glow'	◑ S; 4ft (1.2m); lvs mottled purple; stem spiny; fls red; fr. glossy red; prune l. winter; z. 5.
Carpinus betulus	◑ S; 8ft (2.2m); brown lvs retained through winter; good hedge on stilts; clip in m. summer; z. 4.
Corylus avellana	◑ S; 9ft (3m); lvs pale green serrated; suckering; clip in winter; z. 5.
Cotinus coggygria	○ S; 10ft (3.2m); lvs circular; fls like puffs of smoke; grow informally; z. 5.
Fagus sylvatica	● S; 12ft or more (4m); brown lvs retained through winter; clip in m. summer; z. 5.
Prunus spinosa	○ S; 9ft (3m); fls white, e. spring; fr. black, m. autumn; prune l. autumn to e. winter; z. 5.

8   FLOWERING HEDGES

Berberis stenophylla	◑ S; 9ft (3m); evg.; fls yellow-orange, e. summer; fr. black; trim after flowering; z. 6.
Buddleja alternifolia	○ S; 9ft (3m); dec.; fls purple, m. summer; cut hard back l. winter; z. 6.
Camellia × williamsii 'St Ewe'	◑ D (A); 12ft (4m); evg.; lvs dark glossy green; fls deep pink, e. spring; prune after flowering; z. 8.
Escallonia × rigida 'Donard's Seedling'	○ S; 6ft (2m); evg.; fls white, l. summer; prune e. spring; not fully h.; z. 9.
Hebe speciosa 'Alicia Amherst'	○ S (L); 4ft (1.2m); evg.; fls deep purple blue, m. summer; trim after flowering; not fully h.; z. 7.
Hypericum 'Hidcote'	◑ S; 5ft (1.5m); almost evg.; fls yellow, l. summer; prune m. autumn; z. 5.
Nepeta × faassenii 'Six Hills Giant'	○ S (L); 2ft (60cm); herb.; fls lavender-blue; lvs grey woolly; trim after flowering; z. 6.
Osmanthus delavayi	○ S; 6ft (2m); evg.; fls white, frag., m. spring; prune after flowering; not fully h.; z. 8–9.
Rosa 'Fritz Nobis'	○ S; 5ft (1.5m); fls semi-double, salmon-pink, frag.; hips dark red, persistent; prune e. spring; z. 6.

Rosa 'Madame Isaac Pereire'	○ S; 6ft (2m); fls v. lge, double, crimson, frag., m. summer; prune e. spring; z. 6.
Rosa pimpinellifolia 'Hispida'	○ S; 6ft (2m); fls pale yellow, single, l. spring; hips rounded, prune e. spring; z. 5.
Rosa rugosa 'Roseraie de l'Haÿ'	○ S; 6ft (2m); fls v. lge, semi-double, purplish-crimson, frag., e. summer; prune e. spring; z. 2.
Spiraea 'Argata'	○ S; 6ft (2m); decid.; fls white, e. spring before lvs; prune after flowering; z. 5.
Syringa vulgaris cvs	○ M; 12ft (4m); decid.; fls white to purple, l. spring; prune after flowering, z. 4.
Viburnum opulus 'Sterile'	○ M (L); 6ft (2m), decid., fls white, in round panicles, l. spring; lvs colour in autumn; prune after flowering; z. 3.

9   VIGOROUS CLIMBERS SUITABLE FOR PERGOLAS

Actinidia chinensis	○ S; 30ft (10m); decid.; fls cream-buff; fr. brown; z. 8.
Clematis armandii	◑ M; 20ft (6m); evg.; fls white, frag., l. spring; lvs dark glossy green, z. 8.
Clematis montana	◑ M; 24ft (8m); decid.; fls purple-blue, l. spring (*C.m.* 'Rubens', fls pink); z. 5–6.
Clematis tangutica	○ M; 18ft (5–6m); fls nodding, yellow, l. summer; fr. silky tassels; z. 6.
Hedera colchica 'Dentata Variegata'	◑ S; 16ft (5m); lvs heart-shaped to 20cm long (8in), green with irregular creamy margins; z. 7.
Humulus lupulus 'Aureus'	◑ M; 20ft (6m); twining herb. per.; lvs 3–5 lobed, flushed golden yellow; fls (hops) in clusters, l. summer; z. 7.
Lonicera japonica halliana	◑ S; 24ft (8m); fls white, ageing yellow, frag., m. summer; fr. black; z. 5.
Passiflora caerulea	○ S; 30ft (10m); decid.; fls purple; lvs deeply lobed; fr. orange plum-shaped; not fully h.; z. 7.
Polygonum baldschuanicum	○ S; 45ft (15m); decid.; fls white or pink tinted, m. summer; very invasive; z. 5.
Vitis coignetiae	◑ M; 40ft (13m); lvs 1ft (30cm) long; scarlet and crimson in autumn; fr. black; z. 5.
Wisteria sinensis	○ M; 45ft (15m); decid.; fls purple to 1ft (30cm) long, l. spring, before lvs; z. 5.

10   RAMBLING ROSES

All deciduous and US zone 6–7 unless stated; some winter protection may be needed.

'Alberic Barbier'	○ S; 25ft (8.3m); fls single, in small clusters, white, v. floriferous, m. summer; lvs dark glossy green.
'Albertine'	◑ S; 20ft (6.6m); fls in small clusters, pink, e. summer; suits north wall; v. prickly.
Rosa banksiae	○ S; 30ft (10m); fls creamy-white, e. summer.
Climbing 'Cécile Brunner'	○ S; 20ft (6.6m); fls double, pale pink, in sprays, frag., v. free-flowering, e. summer.
'Félicité Perpétue'	○ S; 20ft (6.6m); fls small, in lge clusters, creamy-white, scented, free-flowering, m. summer; lvs light green.
Rosa filipes 'Kiftsgate'	○ S; 20ft (6.6m); fls lge clusters, single, white with yellow stamens, e. summer; z. 6.
'Francis E. Lester'	○ S; 15ft (5m); fls single, in lge clusters, white, scented e. to m. summer; hips oval, orange-red l. autumn.
'Lawrence Johnston'	○ S; 20ft (6.6m); fls semi-double, yellow, frag., e. summer; lvs glossy green.
'Madame Alfred Carrière'	○ S; 20ft (6.6m); fls lge, double, white frag.,

	free-flowering m. to l. summer; spiny.
'Madame Grégoire Staechelin'	○ S; 15ft (5m); fls semi-double, pink, in lge clusters, e. summer; hips lge, apricot, m. autumn; v. vigorous.
'Mermaid'	○ S; 25–35ft. (8–12m); fls lge, single, pale yellow, recurrent m. summer to e. autumn; lvs dark green; in mild areas evg.
'Wedding Day'	○ S; 25ft (8.3m); fls single, in lge clusters, white, m. summer; thorny; v. vigorous.

11   TREES AND SHRUBS SUITABLE FOR TRAINING

Buxus sempervirens	● D; 6ft (2m); evg. shrub; lvs small, bright green; train as cones and balls, e. summer, slow growing; z. 6.
Cornus alba 'Sibirica'	◑ M; 5ft (1.5m); decid. shrub; fls. z. 2. white; twigs bright red in winter; pollard m. spring; z. 2.
Cornus mas	◑ M; 24ft (8m); decid. shrub; fls pale yellow, l. winter to e. spring, before leaves; fr. red, m. autumn; clipped shape; z. 5.
Cornus stolonifera	◑ M; 5ft (1.5m); decid. shrub; fls white; twigs yellow, good winter colour; pollard m. spring; z. 2.
Crataegus monogyna	○ S; 18ft (6m); decid. tree; fls white, m. spring; fr. red, l. autumn; clipped shape; z. 5.
Eucalyptus gunnii	○ S; 5ft (1.5m); evg. tree; lvs round, glaucous, juvenile, if coppiced in e. spring; z. 9.
Euonymus fortunei 'Emerald Gaiety'	◑ S; 4ft (1.2m); evg. shrub; lvs grey-green, white margin, pink in winter; good as standard; z. 5.
Ilex aquifolium 'Golden Queen'	● S; 9ft (3m); evg. shrub; lvs margined golden yellow; clipped shape; z. 7.
Laburnum × watereri 'Vossii'	○ S; 9ft (3m); decid. tree; fls yellow in long racemes e. summer; winter train into arch; z. 6.
Laurus nobilis	◑ S; 6ft (2m); evg. shrub; lvs dark green; prune to shape m. summer; z. 9.
Platanus orientalis	○ S; decid. tree; when pleached, to 8ft (2.5m); lvs 3–5 lobed; train in winter; z. 6.
Quercus ilex	◑ S; evg. tree; good hedge on stilts to 12ft (4m); z. 8.
Salix alba 'Chermesina'	○ M; 12ft (4m); decid. tree; winter twigs orange; pollard in l. spring; z. 2.
Taxus baccata	● S; 24ft (8m); evg. tree; lvs dark green, small; train into cones, pyramids, etc., e. summer; z. 7.
Tilia × euchlora	○ S; 24ft (8m); decid. tree; lvs deep glossy green; pleach in winter; z. 6.

12   APPLES SUITABLE FOR TRAINING

All US zone 3; grow on dwarfing virus-free rootstock M.9 or MM. 106. Check compatibility for pollination.

'Bramley's Seedling'	Fr. l. autumn to l. winter, green flushed brownish red, keeps well; vigorous; c.
'Discovery'	Fr. l. summer to e. autumn, pale greenish yellow; good flavour; tip-bearing tendency; d.
'James Grieve'	Fr. e. to m. autumn, pale green, soft but rich, juicy; good pollinator; d.
'Lane's Prince Albert'	Fr. l. autumn to e. spring, light green to pale yellow, good flavour; easy, crops regularly; c.
'Lord Lambourne'	Fr. e. autumn to e. winter, pale greenish yellow, flushed red, juicy; produces spurs freely; d.
'Reverend W. Wilks'	Fr. l. summer, keeps well; easy to grow.
'Sunset'	Fr. m. autumn to l. winter, yellow to orange, crisp, juicy; equals 'Cox' but easier; d.

13 PEARS SUITABLE FOR TRAINING

All US zone 6; grow on rootstock Quince A. Check compatability for pollination.

'Beurré Hardy'	Fr. m. autumn sm., round, greenish yellow, delicious rose-water flavour.
'Conference'	Fr. m. to l. autumn, long green, firm, keeps well, honey-flavoured when fresh.
'Doyenné du Comice'	Fr. l. autumn to e. winter, large yellow; needs warm protected site.
'Joséphine de Malines'	Fr. m. to l. winter, round green, marbled brown, fine fresh, v. good flavour.
'Merton Pride'	Fr. m. to l. autumn, pale green marbled brown, exquisite flavour; needs pollinator.
'Williams Bon Chrétien'	Fr. e. autumn, yellow, typical shape, good taste but soft, poor keeper.

14 WINTER AND EARLY SPRING FLOWERS FOR CONTAINERS

Camellia × williamsii 'Donation'	◑ M (A); 6ft (2m); evg. shrub; fls pink; lvs dark glossy green; need abundant watering; z. 8.
Crocus chrysanthus 'Cream Beauty'	○ D; 4in (10cm); bulb; fls creamy yellow, l. winter.
Daphne mezereum	○ S (L); 3ft (1m); decid. shrub; **fls purple, frag.**, e. spring, before lvs; fr. scarlet, autumn.
Erica carnea	◑ S (L); 1ft (30cm); evg. sub-shrub; **fls white to** pink, l. autumn to e. spring; z. 6.
Hyacinthus cvs	○ S; 1ft (30cm); bulb; fls white, blue, **pink**, e. spring.
Iris histrioides 'Major'	○ D (L); 4in (10cm); bulb; fls blue, l. winter, before lvs; weather resistant.
Iris reticulata cvs	○ D; fls blue with orange falls, 4in (10cm), frag., e. spring, before lvs that grow to 1ft (30cm).
Mahonia aquifolium	● S; 5ft (1.5m); evg. shrub; fls golden **yellow**, frag., l. winter; lvs pinnate, prickly; fr. black, l. summer; z. 5.
Narcissus asturiensis	◑ S; 2–4in (5–10cm); bulb; fls miniature yellow trumpet, e. spring.
Narcissus 'February Gold'	◑ S; 1ft (30cm); bulb; cyclamineus hybrid; fls yellow perianth and trumpet, e. spring.
Narcissus 'Tête-à-Tête'	◑ S; 6–8in (15–20cm); bulb; fls pale yellow perianth, orange yellow cup, often in pairs, e. spring.
Primula × tommasinii	◑ S; 6in (15cm); evg. per.; fls yellow, red, pink, purple, white carried on scapes, e. spring.
Viburnum tinus	● D; 3ft (1m); evg. shrub; fls white to pink, l. autumn to e. spring; fr. black blue l. summer to e. autumn; z. 7.
Viola × wittrockiana Majestic Giants	○ S; 6in (15cm); annual; fls blue, red, yellow, white, l. winter.

15 SPRING AND EARLY SUMMER FLOWERS FOR CONTAINERS

Centaurea cyanus	○S; 2ft (60cm); annual; fls blue, white pink, e. summer; sow in l. autumn.
Muscari armeniacum	◑ S; 4–8in (10–20cm); bulb; fls bright blue, white margin, m. spring.
Narcissus triandrus 'Thalia'	◑ S; 14–20in (35–50cm); bulb; fls 2–3 white, hanging, m. to l. spring.
Narcissus 'Professor Einstein'	○ S; 18in (45cm); bulb; fls white perianth, lge orange-red cup, m. spring.
Rhododendron 'Cilpinense'	◑ M (A); 3ft (1m); evg. shrub; fls white, flushed pink, m. spring.
Rhododendron 'Elizabeth'	◑ M (A); 4ft (1.2m); evg. shrub; fls rich dark red, l. spring.

16 SUMMER AND EARLY AUTUMN FLOWERS FOR CONTAINERS

Agapanthus Headbourne Hybrids	○ S; 2ft (60cm); decid. per.; fls blue, purple or white, m. to l. summer; not fully h.
Begonia semperflorens	◑ S; 8in (20cm); annual; fls white to red, summer; lvs can be bronzy; not fully h.
Convolvulus tricolor 'Royal Ensign'	○ S; 1ft (30cm); annual; fls purple-blue, white and yellow eye, m. summer to e. autumn.
Cosmos bipinnatus	○ M; 30in (75cm); annual; fls white to red, l.summer to e. autumn; lvs feathery; sow l. spring.
Diascia rigescens	○ S; 20in (50cm); herb. per.; fls pink, e. summer to e. autumn; not fully h.
Fuchsia magellanica 'Pumila'	○ S; 1ft (30cm); dwarf decid. shrub; fls small, scarlet and mauve; not fully h.
Impatiens 'Novette Mixed'	◑ M; 6in (15cm); annual; fls many shades, e. summer to e. autumn; not fully h.
Lilium auratum	○ S(A); 3ft (1m); bulb; fls white, banded yellow and spotted crimson, l. summer.
Lotus berthelotti	○ S; sub-shrub; trailing to 2 ft (60cm); fls scarlet, e. summer to e. autumn; lvs grey, hairy; not fully h.
Nicotiana affinis	○ S; 3ft (1m); annual; fls white, some cvs scented; not fully h.
Osteospermum ecklonis	○ S; 8in (45cm); per.; fls daisy-like, purple, e. to m. summer; crushed lvs scented; not fully h.
Pelargonium 'Princess of Wales'	○ S; 18in (45cm); sub-shrub; regal type; fls pink, frilled edges and centre white; not fully h.
Pelargonium peltatum	○ S; sub-shrub; trailing to 3ft (1m); lvs ivy-like, some variegated; fls white to red; not fully h.
Salvia farinacea	○ S; 2ft (60cm); annual; fls violet-blue, summer; not fully h.
Tropaeolum majus 'Alaska'	○ D; annual; trailing to 15in (40cm); fls yellow to red; lvs mottled cream.

17 FOLIAGE PLANTS FOR CONTAINERS

Acer palmatum	◑ M (A); sm. tree; lvs 5–7 lobed, scarlet in autumn; fls purplish, m. summer; z. 6.
Agave americana	○ D; 3ft (1m); evg. per.; lvs leathery, grey-green, spiny; not fully h.
Ballota pseudodictamnus	○ S; 2ft (60cm) spread; trailing evg. shrub; lvs round, yellowish, woollen.
Buxus sempervirens	● D; 3ft (1m); evg. shrub; lvs, sm round; z. 6.
Centaurea gymnocarpa	◑ S; 30in (75cm); evg. sub-shrub or as annual; lvs ferny, silvery; fls. purple, m. summer; not fully h.
Fatsia japonica 'Variegata'	◑ S; 5ft (1.5m); evg. shrub; lvs palmate, 1ft (30cm) wide, white margined; not fully h; z. 8.
Hedera helix 'Conglomerata'	● S; stems to 2ft (60cm); evg. per.; lvs v. sm. in 2 tight ranks; forms hummock; z. 5.
Hedera helix 'Marginata'	◑ S; stems to 4ft (1.2m); trailing evg. per.; lvs scarcely lobed, white margined, tinged pink in winter; z. 5.
Helichrysum petiolare	○ D; spreading to 3ft (1m); trailing evg. shrub or as annual; lvs white felted; not fully h.
Laurus nobilis	◑ S; 5ft (1.5m); evg. shrub; best kept clipped; not fully h.; z. 9.
Melianthus major	○ M; 5ft (1.5m); semi-evg. shrub; lvs coarsely toothed, pinnate; not fully h; z. 10.
Pelargonium tomentosum	◑ D; trailing evg. shrub; to 3ft (1m); lvs shallowly lobed, downy, peppermint scented; not fully h.
Phormium tenax	○ D; 5ft (1.5m); lvs stiff, erect, glaucous; not fully h.

BIBLIOGRAPHY

Most books on small gardens currently in print are to be avoided for advice on design, although many are valuable on the subject of practical garden construction and horticulture. Here are some of the books I have found an inspiration.

Hadfield, Miles, *Topiary and Ornamental Hedges: Their History and Cultivation* London, 1971. The only comprehensive guide I know.

Hicks, David, *Garden Design*, London, 1982. An index of good taste in gardening.

Hobhouse, Penelope, *The National Trust Book of Gardening*, National Trust, 1986. Although it deals with large National Trust gardens, this is an immensely practical and well-written book; its approach and basic principles are applicable to small gardens.

Jekyll, Gertrude, *Garden Ornament*, London, 1908. In spite of the grand scale of the gardens she discusses, her attitudes and advice continue to be seminal. Available in modern reprint.

Jekyll, Gertrude, and Weaver, Laurence, *Gardens for Small Country Houses*, London, 1912. The gardens are large by our standards but small in comparison with those before 1920; the book is crammed with ideas still relevant today. Available in modern reprint.

Lloyd, Nathaniel, *Garden Craftsmanship in Yew and Box*, London 1925. A collector's item but invaluable on planting and training.

Verey, Rosemary, *Classic Garden Design: Adapting and Recreating Garden Features of the Past*, New York, 1984. A veritable mine of information, including how to plant a knot garden and plan a *potager*.

ACKNOWLEDGEMENTS

The publisher thanks the following photographers and organizations for their permission to reproduce the photographs in this book: 1 Marijke Heuff (Mr & Mrs Dekker-Fokker, Holland); 2 Marijke Heuff (Mr & Mrs Greve-Verhaar, Holland); 8 Marijke Heuff (Mr & Mrs Bennekom-Scheffer, Holland); 10–11 Marijke Heuff (Mr & Mrs Greve-Verhaar, Holland); 12 Jerry Harpur (designer Valery Stevenson); 13–14 Elizabeth Whiting & Associates/Karl Dietrich Buhler; 15 left Derek Gould; 15 right Jerry Harpur (Michael Branch); 16 left Georges Lévêque; 16 right Jerry Harpur (Jenkyn Place, Bentley); 17 Jerry Harpur (York Gate, Adel, Leeds); 18 Michèle Lamontagne; 19 left Linda Burgess; 19 right Michèle Lamontagne; 20–21 Tania Midgley; 23 Harry Smith Horticultural Photographic Collection; 24 above Michèle Lamontagne; 24 below Ianthe Ruthven; 25 above Michèle Lamontagne; 25 below Jerry Harper (designer Lys de Bray, Wimborne Minister); 26 Camera Press; 28–29 Michèle Lamontagne; 30 Heather Angel/Biofotos; 31 Philippe Perdereau; 32 left Michèle Lamontagne; 32 right Philippe Perdereau; 33 Georges Lévêque; 34 Georges Lévêque; 35 Michèle Lamontagne; 36–37 Marijke Heuff (designer Mien Ruys and Hans Veldhoen, Holland); 38 Jerry Harpur; 38–39 Michèle Lamontagne; 40 Marijke Heuff (Mr & Mrs Dekker-Fokker, Holland); 41–43 Michèle Lamontagne; 44 Georges Lévêque; 45 above Peter Baistow; 45 below Jerry Harpur (Castle Howard); 46–47 Heather Angel/Biofotos; 48 Georges Lévêque (Loup de Viane); 49 Jerry Harpur (Barnsley House, Glos); 50–51 Jerry Harpur; 51 above Peter Baistow; 51 below Michèle Lamontagne; 53 Jerry Harpur (designer Nicholas Ridley); 54 left Jerry Harpur; 54 right Michèle Lamontagne; 55 Michèle Lamontagne; 56–57 Georges Lévêque; 58 Jerry Harpur; 58–59 Jerry Harpur (Corpusty Mill, Norfolk); 59 Michèle Lamontagne; 61 Marijke Heuff (Mr & Mrs Greve-Verhaar, Holland; 62–63 Marijke Heuff; 64 left Jerry Harpur (Peckover House, Wisbech); 64–65 Georges Lévêque; 65 Marijke Heuff (Mr & Mrs Groosenaerts-Miedema, Holland); 66 Pamla Toller/Impact Photos; 67 Jerry Harpur; 68 Michèle Lamontagne; 70–71 Georges Lévêque; 72 left Jerry Harpur (Abbots Ripton); 72–73 Marijke Heuff (Mr & Mrs Dekker-Fokker, Holland); 73 Jerry Harpur (Barnsley House, Glos); 74 Marijke Heuff (Mr & Mrs Gossenaerts-Miedema, Holland); 75 Heather Angel/Biofotos; 76 Jerry Harpur (Hillier & Hilton); 77 above Georges Lévêque; 77 below Ardea London; 78–79 Georges Lévêque; 80 Jerry Harpur (Anne Dexter, Oxford); 80–81 Philippe Perdereau; 81 Harry Smith Horticultural Photographic Collection; 82 left Michèle Lamontagne; 82 right Philippe Perdereau; 83 Marijke Heuff (Mr & Mrs Greve-Verhaar, Holland); 84 left Valerie Finnis; 84 right Michèle Lamontagne; 85 Georges Lévêque; 86 Marijke Heuff (Mien Ruys Dedemsvaart, Holland); 88–89 Clive Boursnell; 90 above Jerry Harpur (Barnsley House, Glos); 90 below Marijke Heuff (Mr & Mrs Dekker-Fokker, Holland); 91 Michèle Lamontagne; 93 Marijke Heuff (Giardini Walda Pairon, Belgium); 95 Marijke Heuff (Mr & Mrs Nieuwen Huys, Holland); 96–97 Michèle Lamontagne; 98 Michèle Lamontagne; 99 left Michèle Lamontagne; 99 right Marijke Heuff (Mr and Mrs Bennekom-Scheffer, Holland); 100 Heather Angel/Biofotos; 101 Philippe Perdereau; 102 Philippe Perdereau; 103 above Georges Lévêque; 103 below Michèle Lamontagne; 104 Marijke Heuff; 106–107 Marijke Heuff (Mr & Mrs Poley-Bom, Holland); 109 above left Philippe Perdereau; 109 above right Jerry Harpur (Hall Place, Leigh, Kent); 109 below Marijke Heuff (Mr & Mrs Brinkworth-Makeham, Holland); 110 Georges Lévêque; 111 Clive Boursnell; 112–113 Georges Lévêque; 114–115 Georges Léveque; 117 above Georges Lévêque; 117 below Pat Hunt; 118 Philippe Perdereau; 119 Marijke Heuff (Mr & Mrs Brinkworth-Makeham, Holland); 120–121 Jerry Harpur; 122 Georges Lévêque; 123 Philippe Perdereau; Dedemsvaart); 124 above left Georges Lévêque; 124 above right Jerry Harpur (Bampton Manor); 124 below Jerry Harpur (Great Comp, Kent); 126 right Michèle Lamontagne; 126 left Georges Lévêque; 127 Phillipe Perdereau; 128–129 Heather Angel/Biofotos; 130 Peter Baistow; 131 Marijke Heuff (Mr Korpadi); 132–133 Georges Lévêque; 135 Jerry Harpur (designer Alan Titchmarsh); 136 Linda Burgess; 137 left Marijke Heuff (designer Yak Ritzen); 137 right Michèle Lamontagne.

INDEX